Marge Helwig
June 2, 1928 - December 19, 1997

MW01201127

A fittii

Of all the things I love in life
one face will still remain
a loving, caring, part of me
to lose this causes pain.
I try to see the happy times
those memories from my day.
I search my mind, my heart, my soul
replay them so they'll stay.
This poem is for my nanny
I love her, oh, so dear
forever a big part of me,
I know she's always near.

Brittany Wiggins
12/12/97

Dedication

To those of you who knew Marge Helwig, you can understand why this book is a memorial to her. To those of you who did not have the privilege of knowing her or the honor of meeting her, your lives will be a little less enriched for not having known such a magnificent lady!

She was not a wirewrapper but a "Wire Person" with a large following nationwide. Her willingness to lecture or teach endeared her to many many people from coast to coast. Marge was the very essence of unselfishness in all that she did. Her willingness to share her time and her ideas was her trademark, and the impact of this sharing, even after her death, still cannot be measured.

Her new book, *Wonderful, Wearable Wire (ISBN 0-9650784-2-6)* is available and continues to offer encouragement and challenges to those who seek something different. Marge's ideas continue to have an enormous impact on the craft industry by virtue of the wig jig and its many new variations.

Marge also had an enormous impact on me. It was she who put me on the innovative trail of the colored magnet wire; many of our meetings at the local fast-food restaurant involved discussions about colored wire and what could be done with it. From then on, all of our sessions were a matter of how to do what, and as usual a host of new ideas surfaced; much of what is in this book is a direct influence of these sessions with Marge. Talented people such as Marge are rare, and I know, beyond all doubt, that the world is a far far better place for her being here in spite of the fact that it was for much too short a time!

A final farewell to Marge appears at the end of this book. Her granddaughter's words mirror the feelings of her husband Glen, and my own feelings. I'm sure they also mirror the feelings of those who still miss her so very much! No one has said it better than Brittany.

Marge–you are always in our thoughts!

Ed Sinclair

HOLIDAY MOODS IN WIRE

An Extended Guide to the Fine Art of Wirewrapping

VOLUME 3

Ellsworth "Ed" Sinclair

© 1999 by Ellsworth E. Sinclair

Published by E.E. Sinclair
PO. Box 2011
Manassas, VA 22110

ISBN 0-9640483-2-9

Library of Congress Catalog
Number 98-90882

First printing 1999

Project Coordination: Craig Nelsen
Rodgers & Nelsen Publishing Co.
Loveland CO

Electronic Prepress:
Teel & Co., Loveland CO

Computer Illustrations: Ben Teel,
Teel & Co., Loveland CO
Tools: William W. Ivers, Denver CO

Editor: Barbara Teel
Teel & Co., Loveland CO

Photography: Mel Schockner
Loveland CO

Portrait of Mr. Sinclair:
James L. Digby, Loveland CO

ELLSWORTH "ED" SINCLAIR

A man of diverse interests, Ed Sinclair studied drama at the Shakespearean Institute at Stratford-on-Avon in 1959, and followed that with a two year stint in the Peace Corps in Liberia, West Africa, where he "taught a little bit of everything including history, literature, and carpentry." He retired in 1986 from a twenty-five year teaching career in Fairfax County, Virginia. Ed Sinclair is a graduate of the University of East Carolina and the University of Virginia.

As a native Virginian, he has spent many hours pursuing his mineral collecting hobby throughout the state. Early experiences involved being Field Trip Chairman (and later President) of the Mineralogical Society of the District of Columbia. He is currently a member of the Northern Virginia Mineral Club. He still collects when time permits. His interest in minerals led him to frequent the gem and mineral shows where he was introduced to wirewrapping. He is a self-admitted "Rock Hound." After a short ten-hour course and a year of practice, he embarked upon the craft show circuit in the mid-1970s, doing craft shows from Gettysburg, Pennsylvania to Asheville, North Carolina. Also at that time he served two terms as President of the Northern Virginia Handcrafters Guild, of which he is still an active member.

Ed Sinclair

In recent years Ed has published two successful wirewrap "How to" books previous to this third volume. Even more recently, Ed has become a familiar fixture demonstrating wirewrapping at the Catalog-in-Motion show in Tucson, Arizona. Every February, he can be found there at the Hilton Hotel under the sponsorship of Rio Grande.

Just this year he signed a contract with ACN-TV (American Collectibles Network) in Knoxville, Tennessee. He will be making periodic appearances about once a month, making wirewrap instructional tapes, and making plans for a wirewrap workshop.

Currently, Ed lives in Manassas, Virginia, with his family. He does a limited number of shows every year. Plans are to continue writing wirewrap books as long as his ideas continue to flow!

Mr. Sinclair is available for personal appearances and seminars. He will do demonstrations anytime for expenses including room, board and transportation. Classes are extra. Please call 1-888-337-9474 for fees and schedule arrangements.

INTRODUCTION

*C*reative self-expression is the motivation that drives our imagination. Ideas bridge the gap between mind and hand with a gentle nudge of patience, perseverance and, above all, PRACTICE. These ideas begin to manifest themselves through the discipline of shape and form as beautiful works of art; disciplined creativity is the universal language of any true artisan and is recognized as such. Wirewrapping is no exception to this, and it offers a truly endless variety of possibilities.

In Volume III, (as in Vol. I and Vol. II), the simple easy projects are in the beginning of the book. I would encourage you to master these "easy" projects first. This will help you to get used to the wire and develop a "comfort" zone in which to work more effectively with the wire. You may have a more difficult time if you start in the middle or near the end of the book unless you are an experienced wirewrapper.

Some of the projects in Volume III *look* very complicated. Do not be intimidated by their complexity; each project is a series of very simple steps, and when these simple steps are all put together, the project may look complicated. It is very important to approach the projects in this book with a positive, one step-at-a-time attitude. IT CANNOT BE EMPHASIZED ENOUGH JUST HOW IMPORTANT PRACTICE IS! You must develop a strong sense of mental discipline in order to combat the frustration, which will (at times), surely come. Remember, make the wire do your bidding and at the same time be firm (but gentle), persistent (but gentle).

Make sure you are willing to stay on the path to completion regardless of what obstacles lie ahead. If frustration becomes too great, then put the project down for awhile and take a break. Remember, Rome wasn't built in a day! Wirewrapping is fun, and it can give you a tremendous sense of accomplishment.

PREFACE

Volume III of this wirewrap trilogy will be a wholly new dimension and a new direction in wirewrapping. I call it "Playing with the Wire." Recent discoveries of new materials and a new tool have made it possible to go beyond the confines of everyday, ordinary wirewrapping. There is a lot of fun in jewelry making (Vol. I and II), but Vol. III is, without a doubt, a new horizon of sheer ecstasy which is vibrant with new shapes, new colors, new designs and new ideas!

Wirewrapping is a widely practiced art. Many different systems are employed by many wirewrappers. Expressed in this book are many systems of my own plus variations I have seen or learned. It is not my intention in this book to copy, duplicate, plagiarize, or infringe upon any existing copyrighted materials. Any resemblance is purely coincidental and unintentional. Also, a timely reminder from my "left-handed advisor" Grant Hodges–if you are a lefty, reverse directions.

TABLE OF CONTENTS

BASIC TOOLS FOR WIREWRAPPING

CHAPTER 1 — BASIC TOOLS FOR WIREWRAPPING

#1 INTRODUCTION OF A NEW TOOL

The new tool I would like to introduce is the Twister Pliers. Their formal name is Electric Safety Pliers or Airplane Pliers. When I saw them in a catalog, I immediately thought I had found a way to twist gold-filled and sterling silver wire together—WRONG! The alloy in the gold-filled wire would break before it was twisted sufficiently with the silver. It was then that I discovered the many many combinations of colored wire that can be twisted together and pure inspiration followed!

These pliers have a built-in spinning frame. Here is how they work:

Twister Pliers

- Cut 3 strands of 20 GA round colored wire, 18 to 20 feet long. Each wire should be a different color.

- Fasten one end of each wire to a hook (or vise). Make sure they are very secure. Put the wires together as close to each other as possible making sure there are no kinks, bends, tangles, etc.

- Likewise with the other end (making sure there is no slack in any wire).

- Lock these ends in the pliers. Tug gently to make sure they are even and secure. Support the pliers by a loose grip with the left hand and pull the spinner rod with the right hand. If you are left-handed, switch. The left hand, which is supporting the pliers, is opened enough to let the pliers spin. When the spinner rod is pulled to its maximum, let it go and at the same time grip the pliers tightly with the left hand while the spinner rod retreats to the starting position in the pliers.

This procedure is repeated over and over again (250 to 400 times). An electric drill will do the same job, but with the twister pliers, there is much more control! Up to 6 wires can be twisted together in this manner. If shorter wires are being twisted, it is not necessary to pull it this much. Just remember, the more pulls, the more twists; the more twists, the finer the color pattern. It is a good idea to keep a good supply of tricolored 18'-20' coils in inventory, so when there is a need for some miniature trees, birdcages, or candy canes, there will be a good supply available to make them quickly.

#2 EQUIPMENT

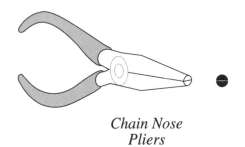

*Chain Nose
Pliers*

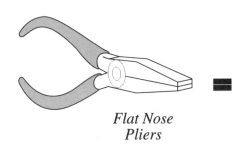

*Flat Nose
Pliers*

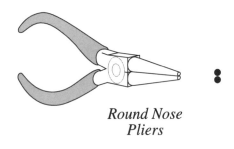

*Round Nose
Pliers*

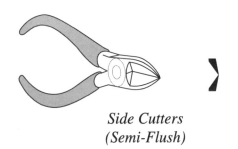

*Side Cutters
(Semi-Flush)*

Pliers: All pliers should be the 4" size.

Chain Nose Pliers: These pliers are similar to the tapered round nose pliers except these pliers have a flat surface on the inside of the jaws. These pliers are used to tuck in ends of wires. They provide a real good grip to forcefully handle the wire without scratching it. They are also used to force the end of the wire through extremely tight places.

Flat Nose Pliers: These pliers are used to bend over ends of wrap wires, crimp ends together, hold wires while bending, straighten bent wires, flatten wire, and hold groups of wires flat.

Round Nose Pliers: These pliers are similar to the chain nose pliers except these are tapered a little more and have no flat surface to grip the wire. These pliers are used to make various sizes of loops. They can also be used to tuck in ends and are very useful when making earrings.

Side Cutters: Used for cutting the wire.

Pin Vise: Used for twisting wire. It is adjustable to all sizes of wire. The wire is passed through the vise. Tighten the vise on the wire just tight enough to still slide it. Make sure the end of the wire nearest the head of the vise is held securely. Tug gently on the vise as you twist the wire. Take no more than 1/4" - 1/2" bites. The number of twists will determine if you have a fine or coarse pattern. **IT IS IMPORTANT TO REMEMBER THAT TOO MANY TWISTS CAN BREAK THE WIRE.**

Pin Vise

Calipers: Used to measure the size of stones for rings (so wrap wires can be accurately placed).

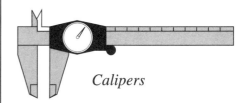

Calipers

Jeweler's Vise: A very small bench vise 4" or smaller is used in making bracelets and other jobs you will discover.

Ring Mandrel: (Grooved or ungrooved) Used for sizing rings.

18" Steel Ruler: (Corked back) Used for measuring wire and making other measurements. (not pictured)

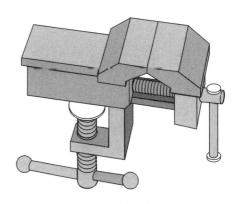

Jeweler's Vise

Small Pocket Knife: (With pointed blade) Point is used to create small openings for wire to be forced through. (not pictured)

Jeweler's File: For filing down rough edges of cut wire. (not pictured)

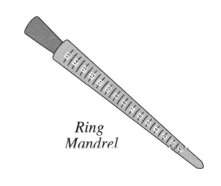

Ring Mandrel

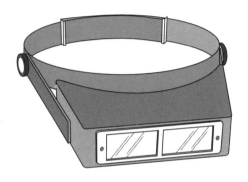

Opti-Visor

Ring Sizer Set

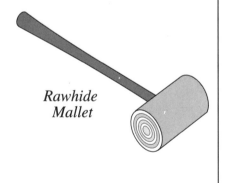

Rawhide Mallet

Opti-Visor: For magnification — especially when making free form rings.

Ring Sizer Set: For measuring fingers. **MAKE SURE THE RING SIZES ARE CALIBRATED WITH THE RING MANDREL.**

Plastic or Leather Hammer: Used for shaping rings on the mandrel and for making bracelets.

Compartmented Box: Wood, plastic, or metal for storing odds and ends. Should be at least 12" x 12" with eight to ten compartments. (not pictured)

Twister Pliers: Used for twisting lengths of wire. Also known as Electric Safety Pliers. These pliers have a built-in spinning frame.

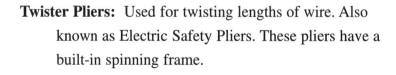

Twister Pliers

CHAPTER 2

MATERIALS

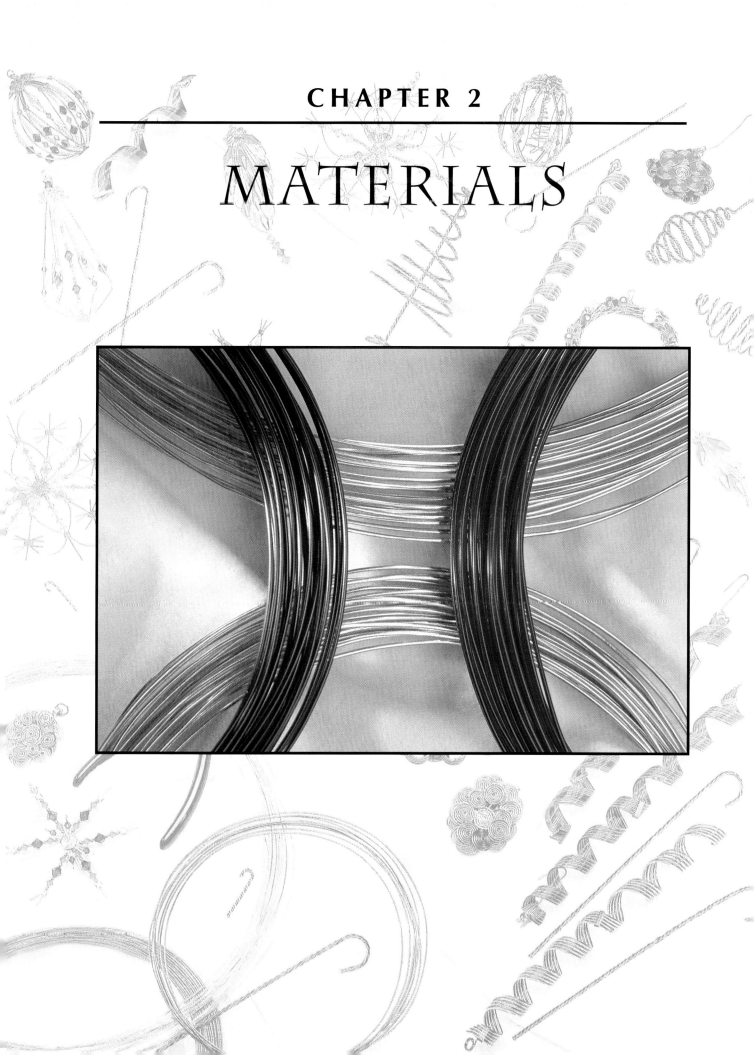

18

#1 INTRODUCTION OF NEW WIRE

The new material I refer to is called Magnet Wire. This wire is used primarily for wrapping armatures in electric motors and must be insulated so as not to short out the motor. Magnet wire therefore is covered with a thin layer of polyurethane insulation, and is usually red. Other colors are available. I use mostly red, green, along with brass and silver-colored craft wire. I use mostly round magnet wire, 20 GA and 22 GA. It is available only in dead soft (not 1/2 hard or full hard). Multiple strands, twisted together, can be used for many projects. Small spools of magnet wire can be obtained at your local hardware store or electrical supply store. Silver and gold-colored craft wire can be purchased at local craft supply stores.

Square magnet wire is available at wholesale electrical supply stores. However, it is expensive and minimum quantity amounts are required for purchase. Square magnet wire, in spite of being dead soft, has a good temper to it and can be twisted easily with a pin vise. I would discourage using magnet wire for making rings. The coating of polyurethane will show signs of wear in a short time. Earrings and decorator items not subject to such wear and abrasion are no problem.

Working with magnet wire is not easy. It's like working with Teflon-coated wire. With patience and practice, beautiful ornaments can be made. The advantage of magnet wire over niobium wire: Niobium wire is colored by electroplating. It is difficult to handle this electroplated wire without scratching it even by using padded pliers. Damaged niobium wire is not easily repaired. Magnet wire, which has a polyurethane covering, presents no such problem. It can be handled easily (no padded pliers). Just be careful when using a pin vise. It can take several days to get used to magnet wire, but once you get the feel of it, beautiful things can happen!

#1 Wire (continued)

A. Wire for Finished Ornaments:

Gold-Filled Wire

20 gauge (.032)

22 gauge (.025)

Sterling Silver Wire

20 gauge (.032)

22 gauge (.025)

Brass Wire

Round, non-tarnishable. Can be purchased at your
local lapidary, craft, or hardware store.

20 gauge (.032)

22 gauge (.025)

24 gauge (.020)

Square, (practice wire). Can be purchased at your
local lapidary store or from jewelry related
catalogs.

Copper Wire

Round

18 gauge (.040)

20 gauge (.032)

22 gauge (.025)

24 gauge (.020)

Square

21 gauge (.028)

22 gauge (.025)

Can be purchased at your local lapidary
store or from jewelry related catalogs.

Magnet Wire

      Round

            20 gauge (.032)

            22 gauge (.025)

      Square

            20 gauge (.032)

            22 gauge (.025)

B.   Inexpensive Wire

Local hardware stores and electrical supply stores are a "treasure house" of all different types and sizes of good inexpensive wire—everything from copper, zinc, to aluminum. Be brave. **EXPERIMENT**!!!

#2 BEADS

A.   Glass Beads: 4mm to 12mm. A wide variety of other bead material is available at your local craft store.

    1. Swarofsky beads

    2. Czech beads

    3. French glass beads

B.   Mineral Beads

    1. Gold-filled 2mm beads

    2. Sterling silver 2mm beads

    3. Copper beads 3mm

#3 MISCELLANEOUS

    A.   Jeweler's cloth

    B.   Piece of felt 12" x 18"

    C.   Small work table

    D.   Two small plastic boxes with lids (for scrap wire)

    E.   Fine line felt tip pen

    F.   Small roll of paper tape

    G.   Cotton bags (for wire)

    H.   A small carrying case (for tools and wire)

CHAPTER 3

CANDY CANES

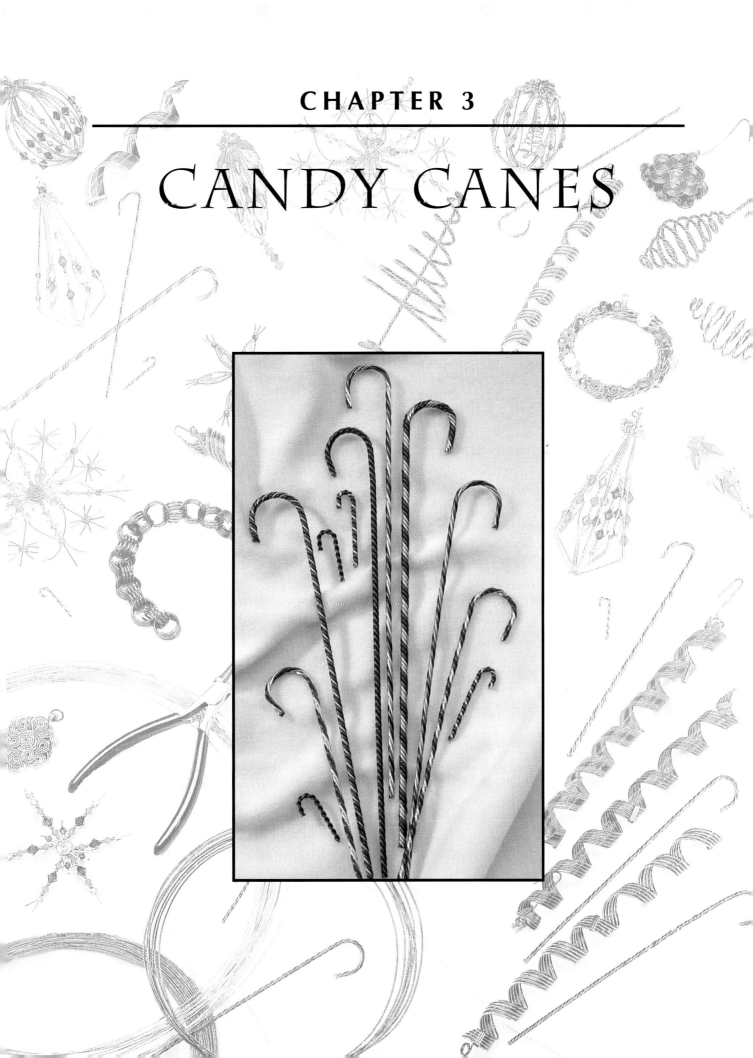

24

#1 CANDY CANES

Materials Needed:

　　1 length of 3 wires (twisted together) 15' to 18' long (20 GA). This length should produce about 2 dozen 6" candy canes. How to twist such a length is explained in Chapter 1, page 13.

Tools Needed:

　　Ruler: 12" to 18" long

　　1/2" wooden dowel

　　wire cutters

Procedure:

A.　Each coil of wire you have twisted will have at either end of it a 1" or 1 1/2" of untwisted wire which was used to secure it to a hook and the other end clamped in the twister pliers. These wires can be snipped off 1 or 2 inches below where they blend together. (There is a reason for such a generous cut.) SAVE THE ENDS. Do not throw them away! *See Diagram 1.*

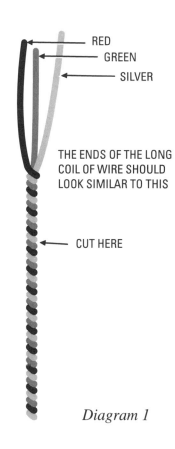

RED

GREEN

SILVER

THE ENDS OF THE LONG COIL OF WIRE SHOULD LOOK SIMILAR TO THIS

CUT HERE

Diagram 1

B.　After you have snipped off these ends, wrap, very carefully, the most convenient end, halfway or 3/4" around the 1/2" wooden dowel so it resembles a hook with the end pointing in slightly. *See Diagram 2.*

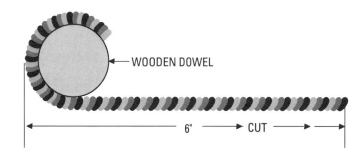

WOODEN DOWEL

6"　　CUT

Diagram 2

C.　Measure 6" from the top of the cane and cut. The cane should be a total of 6" long.

D.   If you feel uncomfortable about working with one end of a very long coil of wire, then cut the rest of the coil in 7" lengths and bend one end of each 7" length around the wooden dowel as in *Diagram 2.*

E.   Repeat Step B or Step D instructions until the entire length of the tricolor coil of magnet wire is used up. If there is a short piece left, save it in a box for tricolored scraps.

#2 "WHATEVERS"

SUGGESTED DESIGNS FOR "WHATEVER" EARRINGS MADE FROM WHATEVER IS LEFT FROM A 3 WIRE COIL

The pieces mentioned in Step A on the previous page can also go into this box. This is what I call a "Whatever" box. From this box there will be a constant flow of "Whatever earrings" from *whatever* is left from the tricolor coils of magnet wire. You can really use your imagination on these "Whatever" scraps in making new and different designs. Using these instructions (for candy canes), you can also use 22 GA wire for miniature candy cane earrings and very fragile birdcage ornaments.

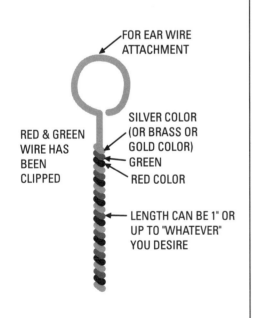

FOR EAR WIRE ATTACHMENT

SILVER COLOR (OR BRASS OR GOLD COLOR)

RED & GREEN WIRE HAS BEEN CLIPPED

GREEN

RED COLOR

LENGTH CAN BE 1" OR UP TO "WHATEVER" YOU DESIRE

"Whatever" 1

A.   Additional Information:
  1. Magnet wire can be mixed with most other craft wire of the same gauge.
  2. Candy canes can be made with 3 wires, 4 wires, 5 wires, or 6 wires—more than 6 wires and you are on your own.

B. **The most popular color combinations are:**

Red, green, silver

Red, green, brass

Red, green

Red, silver

Green, silver

Red, brass (gold color)

Green, brass

There are other colors out there—go to it!

C. Make sure all finished canes are straight!

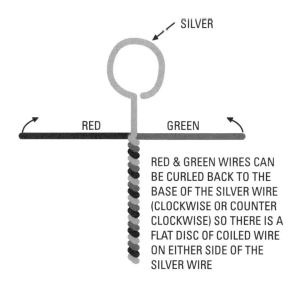

RED & GREEN WIRES CAN BE CURLED BACK TO THE BASE OF THE SILVER WIRE (CLOCKWISE OR COUNTER CLOCKWISE) SO THERE IS A FLAT DISC OF COILED WIRE ON EITHER SIDE OF THE SILVER WIRE

FOR MORE THAN THREE WIRES, MORE FLAT DISCS OF COILED WIRE CAN BE SPACED AROUND THE TOP OF THE EARRING IN A DECORATIVE MANNER

"Whatever" 2

CHAPTER 4

MINI TRICOLOR CHRISTMAS TREES

#1 CHRISTMAS TREES

The original concept for this tree was originated by my "left-handed advisor" Grant Hodges. It's a very sound concept, and after a few prototypes, the base and ratio proportions (to height) were worked out by yours truly.

Materials Needed: (For 1 small tree)
1. 1 26" length of tricolored wire
   (Remember: Tricolored wire is three wires, each a different color, twisted together to form one wire.)

2. Ruler-12" to 18"

3. Wire cutters

4. Round nose pliers

5. Flat nose pliers

A.   Bend 6" from one end so that the 6" part is at a right angle (90 degrees) to the rest of the wire. *See Diagram 3.*

B.   Using the smallest part of the round nose pliers (the tip), grip the 20" part of the wire at the base of the 6" part of the wire so that it appears that the 6" wire is protruding from the jaws of the pliers. *See Diagram 4.*

C.   Then bend the 20" wire over the top of the jaws of the pliers and down the other side of the pliers. *See Diagram 5.* Switch the other jaw to the base of the vertical wire so a complete circle can be made around it.

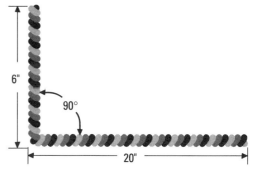
Diagram 3

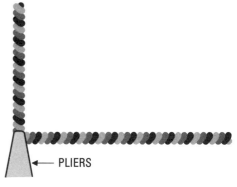

PLIERS

Diagram 4

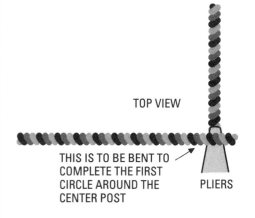

TOP VIEW

THIS IS TO BE BENT TO COMPLETE THE FIRST CIRCLE AROUND THE CENTER POST

PLIERS

Diagram 5

PLIERS REMOVED

Diagram 5A

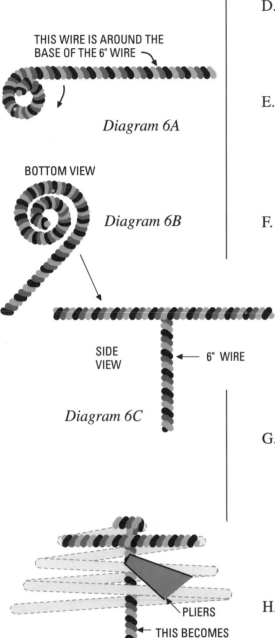

THIS WIRE IS AROUND THE
BASE OF THE 6" WIRE

Diagram 6A

BOTTOM VIEW

Diagram 6B

SIDE
VIEW   ← 6" WIRE

Diagram 6C

PLIERS

THIS BECOMES
THE "TRUNK" OF
THE TREE (AS WELL
AS THE PLATFORM)

Diagram 7

D.   Continue to wrap the 20" wire around the base of the 6" wire so that it forms a flat disk. *See Diagrams 6A and 6B.*

E.   As the flat disk grows larger, hold it with the flat nose pliers or with the hand that is not doing the wrapping. Try to keep the flat disk as tight as possible until the 20" wire is all used up.

F.   You now have a flat disk of wire with a 6" wire in the center, perpendicular to it. *See Diagram 6C.*

G.   Grip the 6" wire with the flat nose pliers, making sure the flat disk is on top and gently (but firmly) push up so that the first coil of the disk is above the rest of the disk. *See Diagram 7.* The second and third coils will also come up a little bit too—don't worry.

H.   When the first coil of the disk is raised above the rest to the disk, the first coil can now be gripped by the flat nose pliers.

I.   By pulling on this first coil, gently, each coil can be
      pulled separate from the disk so it becomes an inverted
      spiral cone with a shaft in the center. *See Diagram 8.*

J.   It is not easy to make (shape) this spiral cone, but with
      gentle and firm manipulation, it can be done. Try to
      make the spirals as parallel to each other as possible
      while maintaining, as much as possible, a cone shape.
      Do not spread them apart too much.

K.   When the cone is finished, the center post (trunk) can be
      centered by gripping the top loop again and manipulat-
      ing it so the "trunk" is centered in the middle of the
      cone.

L.   Bend the "trunk" of the "tree" 90 degrees, 1" below the
      last coil of the tree. *See Diagram 9.*

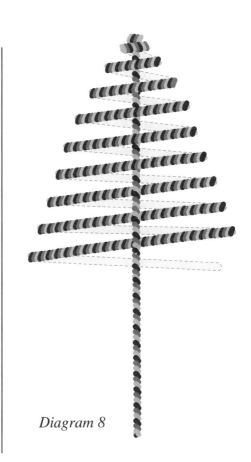

Diagram 8

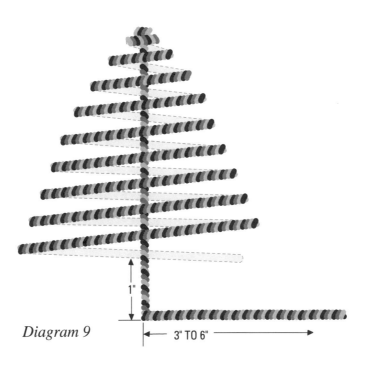

Diagram 9 |← 3" TO 6" →|

1"

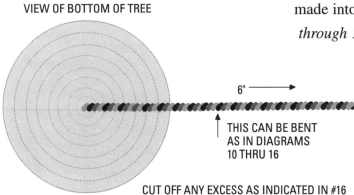

VIEW OF BOTTOM OF TREE

6"

THIS CAN BE BENT
AS IN DIAGRAMS
10 THRU 16

CUT OFF ANY EXCESS AS INDICATED IN #16

M.   The remaining wire (3" to 4") after the bend can be made into a "tree stand." *See Diagrams 10 through 16.* **Use the flat nose pliers.**

N.   Make sure the "trunk" of the tree is perpendicular to the 4 feet (legs) of the platform. It can be done!

O.   Common sense will dictate where the flat nose pliers are to be placed to make the necessary bends.

P.   All bends are to be 90 degrees or 180 degrees! (Bend appropriately.)

Q.   Each "foot" of the tree stand is about 1/2" to 3/4" long.

R.   In each of these drawings (10 through 16) the bottom view only is shown.

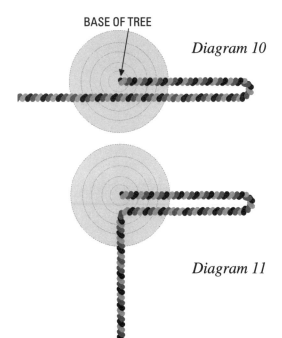

BASE OF TREE

Diagram 10

Diagram 11

S.   The length of each "foot" of this base is determined by the height of the tree. Each "foot" should be 1/2" to 3/4" long if the "tree" is less than 3 1/2" tall. If the tree is taller than 3 1/2" add 1/2" to each "foot" of the base.

T.   On a 5"or 6" tree, each "foot" should be 1 1/2" to 2" long.

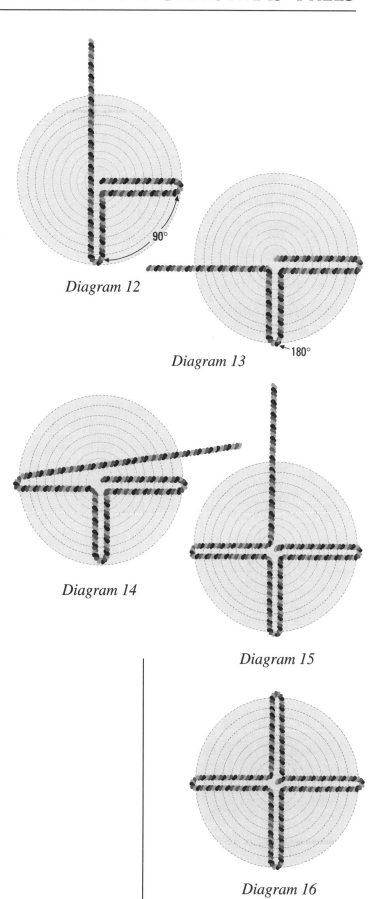

Diagram 12

Diagram 13

Diagram 14

Diagram 15

Diagram 16

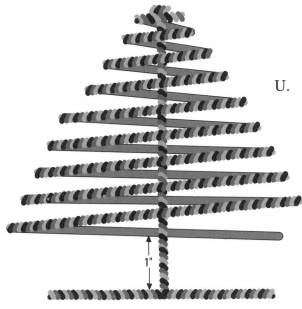

Finished Tree

U.   Remember that the more trees you make, the easier it
      becomes!

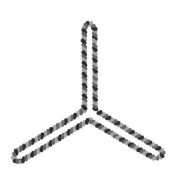

3 Prong Foot Base

V.   For 5" to 6" trees, you may make a 3 prong "foot"
      base.

W.   The "body" of the tree can be separated (spread apart)
      further than the drawing indicates.

CHAPTER 5

MINI CHRISTMAS WREATHS

38

#1 CHRISTMAS WREATHS

Materials:

1. You will need a length of tricolored wire (three wires, each a different color, twisted together) 36" or 60" long. (If you want a "skinny" wreath, use the shorter length; for a thicker wreath, use the longer length.)

2. An assortment of beads (red-silver-green-gold, etc.) 2 to 6 mm in size. (15-20 each)

3. Short 3" lengths of colored wire (about 6 or 8) (swirls).

4. (Optional) An assortment of silver/gold-filled head-pins (can be used to fasten beads to wreath) 1/2" to 3/4" long.

Procedure:

A. Tie a simple loose overhand knot in the wire so there is an equal amount of unused wire on either side of the knot. Pull either end so the circle that is formed is about 1 3/4" to 2" in diameter. *See Diagram 17.*

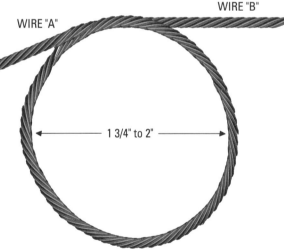

WIRE "A" WIRE "B"

1 3/4" to 2"

Diagram 17

B. Keeping in mind the diameter of the wreath, and using the first loop as a guide, take the end of Wire "A" and put it though the back of the first loop, and pull it through so the rest of wire follows the contour of the first loop.

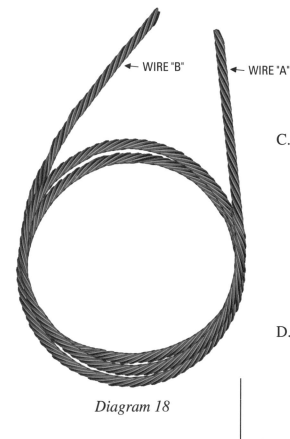

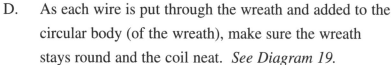

Diagram 18

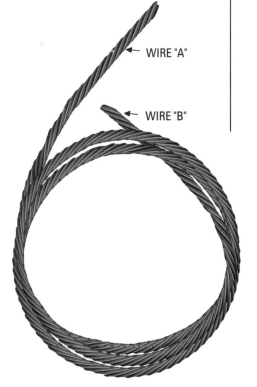

Diagram 19

C.   Do likewise with Wire "B" only put the end of the wire through the front of the loop. *See Diagram 18.* Keep as round as possible.

D.   As each wire is put through the wreath and added to the circular body (of the wreath), make sure the wreath stays round and the coil neat. *See Diagram 19.*

E.   Continue Steps B and C and D until all the wire is used. The last inch or two of each wire can be wrapped, neatly, around the wreath and the end tucked in permanently—it has to be well-hidden. *See Diagram 20.*

Diagram 20

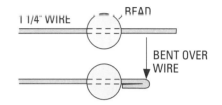

Diagram 21

Diagram 22

Diagram 23

F.   If you are really creative, make a wire bow (the same way you tie your shoelaces) and secure it to the wreath when it is finished.

G.   You may now fill the wreath with all sorts of "goodies." (Beads and coils of wire and any other ideas.) The procedure is as follows:

H.   You will need a 1 1/4" piece of wire to attach each bead (or 1 1/2" head pin).

I.   Drawings are enlarged for clarity. *Diagram 21* shows using a 1 1/4" wire—bend over one end as shown (to prevent the bead from slipping off). The other end of this wire is wrapped around *one* tricolored wire in the wreath very snugly.

J.   *Diagram 22* shows the use of a headpin. Secure it to the wreath as in Step I.

K.   You may want to use 12 to 15 beads, mostly red, green, clear, brass, silver, or gold color spaced evenly around the wreath.

L.   Also in between the beads you can add several coils of different colored wire. *See Diagram 23.* Start with a 3" piece of wire for each coil—leave at least 1/2" to 3/4" wire at the end so it can be used to tie the coil to the wreath.

M.   You can make a large and thick jump ring around the top of the wreath so you can insert a hook, which can be used to hang it from the tree. *Diagram 24.*

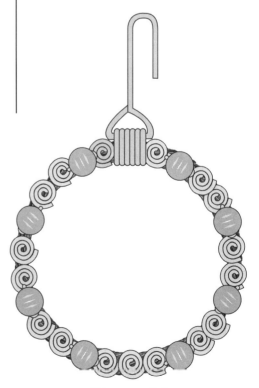

Diagram 24

41

#2 SOLID MINI WREATHS

The following directions for pendant and earrings first appeared in Volume II, *Moods in Brass & Glass,* pages 61 and 62, and have been included here in modified form for your convenience. They can be adapted for Holiday usage by using the appropriately colored wire as shown in the photo introducing this chapter.

A. These directions are for the pendant AND the earrings. The only difference is the length and number of wires being dealt with.

B. It is also important to note that when making earrings, in order to have them reasonably well matched, they must be made together; I would advise this set be made together so that each wire, when coiled, can be put in the identical same place on the other earring. Just alternate each earring with the other, wire by wire for accuracy of design and matching similarity.

C. There will be no separate directions for the earrings because they are made exactly like the pendant. There are, however, other options for the pendant. For a small pendant (approximately 1" in diameter when finished) use fifteen wires 6" long. For a larger pendant (approximately 1 1/2" in diameter when finished) use fifteen wires 10" long. If a larger pendant is desired, increase the length of the wires by 5". *Diagram A* Suggested color combinations are:

    1. brass, red, green
    2. silver, red, green
    3. red, green

13 OR 15 WIRES
TIED TOGETHER
WRAP WIRE COVER
IS TWISTED SQUARE

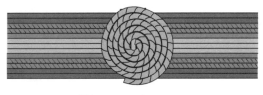

Diagram A

WRAP WIRE COLOR
SUGGESTIONS.
GOLD, SILVER,
RED, OR GREEN

Make sure this group of wires is held together by a wrap wire in the exact center. Also add to this wrap wire a cover on both sides. See instructions for wrap wire cover in Chapter 11, pages 79-82.
Experiment! It's a lot of fun!!!

D. For design appeal, different textures and colors intermixed are very desirable; therefore random twisting of some of the square wires (before being coiled into a disk) is a must. It is a good contrast when they are interspersed with plain coils, especially when arranged in a circle.

E. If it is done correctly, there is no front or back to this pendant.

F. Another appealing design would be to put 2mm beads at the center of a few or all of the flat disk coils.

G. It is also important to note that the wires closest to the center of the group can be shortened 1/2" to 1" before being twisted and coiled into flat disks.

H. As the coiling process begins, start with the inside wires and surround the wrap wire (on BOTH sides) first. This sets the pattern for the entire pendant. In the center of the pendant there will be 6 flat disks on one side and 7 on the other side spaced so as to surround the wrap wire. (There will be 7 on one side because the exact center wire is the other end of the wire to be utilized as a hanger which will be made into a round jump ring for a chain to pass through, or a hook for an ornament.).

THIS WIRE TO BE ROLLED INTO A JUMP RING FOR A CHAIN TO PASS THROUGH. FOR A TREE ORNAMENT, A HOOK CAN BE MADE.

Diagram B

Diagram C

I.   Note the photo of this pendant on page 37 to get a better idea of what you are to do and the color options. When the center wires are completed, you now have a half-finished pendant. It looks like a small round "Oreo cookie", part of it consisting of half of the disks on either side with the middle "goodies" consisting of the wrap wire from which radiate the rest of the wires. *Diagram B*

J.   The reverse side looks identical except for half of the disks as explained earlier. The remaining wires are shown as every other one twisted. These wires can be rolled as indicated and placed tightly between the sandwiched coils already completed. *Diagram C*

K.   Just a reminder: Earrings are done the same way, just on a smaller scale.

These solid mini wreaths make delightful ornaments or decorations and may also be worn as pendants and earrings in the off season as wearable art.

CHAPTER 6

TREE GARLANDS

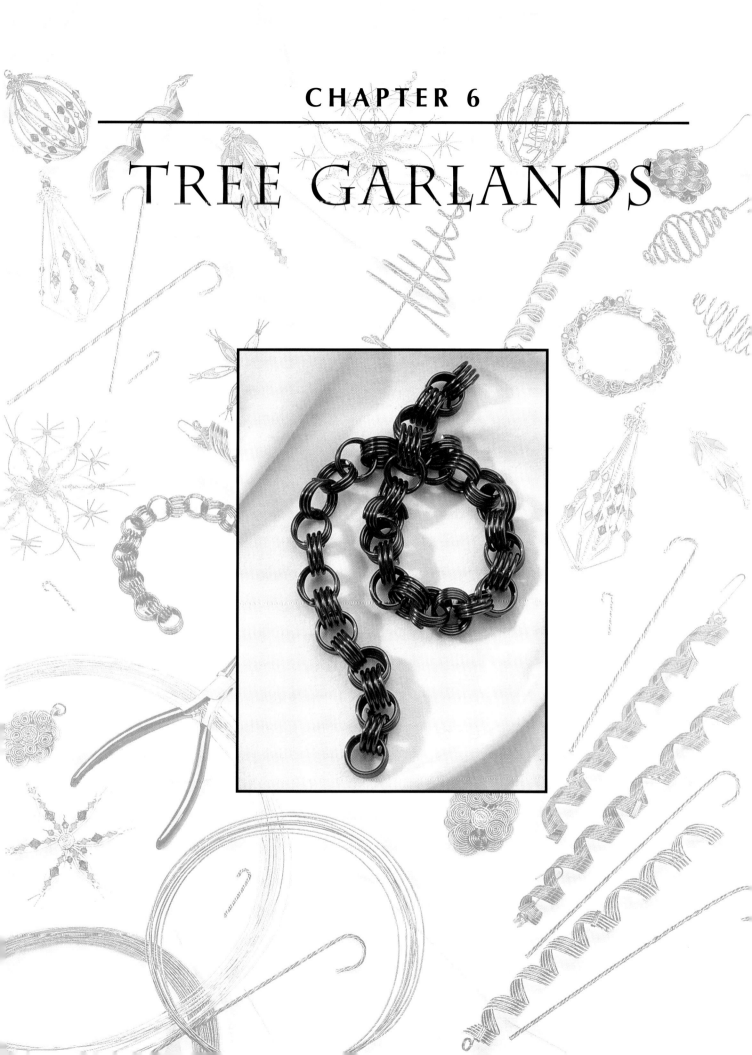

#1 TREE GARLANDS

A.   Tree Garlands are, without a doubt, "frosting on the cake" for tree decorations. They are a lot of fun to make because of a lesser degree of difficulty. Keep in mind that they are usually a minimum of 10 to 15 feet long.

B.   For those of you unfamiliar with garlands, just think of them as giant chains. The links can be of any size or shape. The most popular shapes are round, rectangular, and triangular.

C.   The easiest and quickest way to make these shapes is to go to your local hardware store and check the molding department. There is a wide variety of shapes and sizes available. Select the shapes you want (or the ones mentioned above) and purchase a 3 foot section of each, or as a beginning, just purchase a short round dowel of a desired diameter (above 1/2"). Drill a small hole in it (1/8") 1" from one end perpendicular to the center plane. *See Diagram 25.*

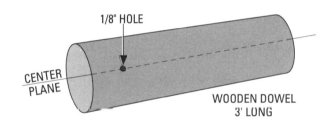

Diagram 25

D.   Cut a piece of wire 6 to 8 feet in length. This wire can be 18 GA, or 20 GA or 21 GA.

E.   Insert one end of the wire in the 1/8" hole. This will serve to hold the end of the wire in place as you wind the wire in close coils around the dowel. Wind them as close to each other as possible. Continue to wind until all of the wire is used. *See Diagram 26.*

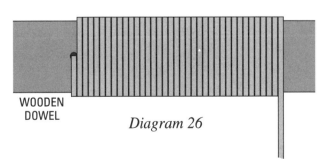

Diagram 26

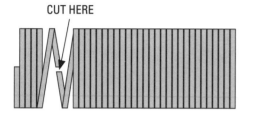

Diagram 27

F. With the wire cutters, clip the end of the wire where it goes into the 1/8" hole.

G. Slide the coil of wire off the dowel. It should resemble a long spring (like the old screen door springs).

H. Count off 4 turns and cut as indicated in *Diagram 27*.

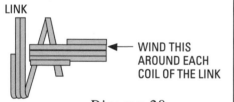

Diagram 28

Diagram 29

I. Repeat this step until the entire coil is used.

J. The length of the garland will determine how many times you have to repeat Steps D through I.

K. When you have a sufficient number of links, they can be joined together as follows:

L. Starting with 2 links, insert one of the ends of one link in between the coils of the other link and turn it until all of the coils (of the link being inserted) are totally encompassed, (only then will they be linked together). *See Diagrams 28 and 29.*

M.   Repeat Step L until all of the links are used.

N.   This same process can be done by using triangular or rectangular molding or any other shape your imagination dictates.

O.   The most popular color is red wire used with silver-colored craft wire. Using three different colors is very popular also. Shorter garlands can be used in other holiday decorations. Colored candy canes can also be hung from them. Let your imagination GO!

P.   Other suggested color combinations are on page 55 in Chapter 7.

CHAPTER 7

SNOWFLAKE TREE GARLANDS

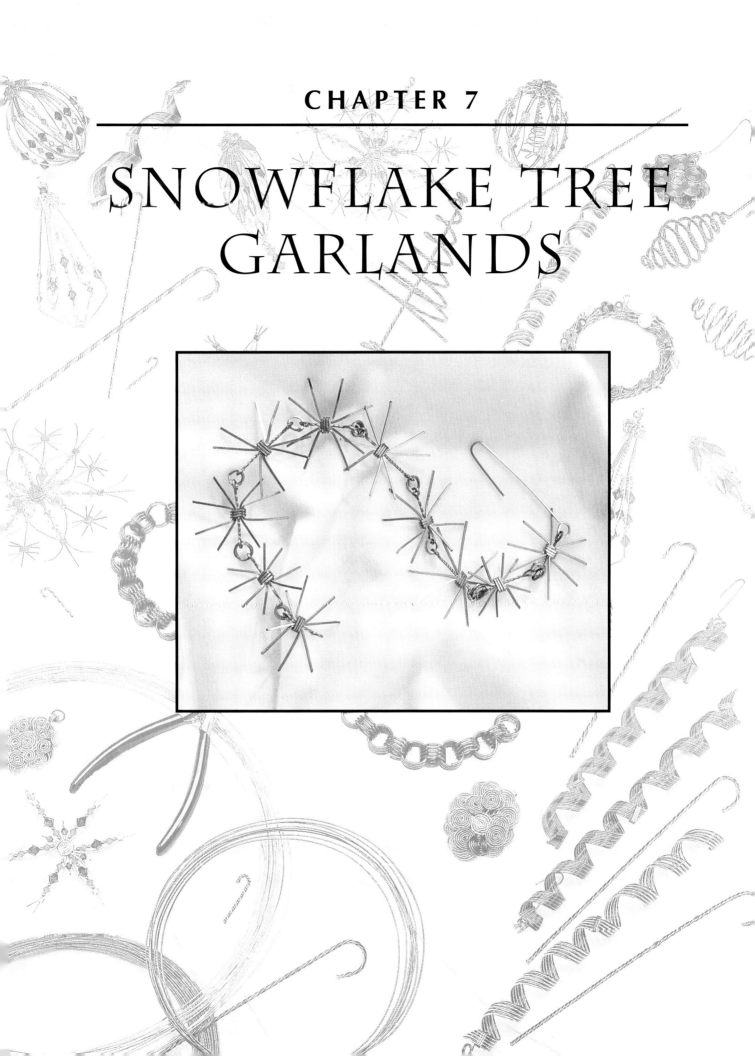

#1 SNOWFLAKE GARLANDS

This is the easiest to make and the most versatile of all the tree decorations. It has countless uses. This garland can be taken apart easily, and the "links" can be used for a wide variety of novel items that will be suggested at the end of this chapter. Have fun!!!

A.   Use square wire only! 21 GA or 22 GA wire.

B.   Cut one wire 3" long and twist it.

C.   Cut 6 wires 1" long (do not twist).

D.   Cut 1 wire 2" long.

E.   Arrange them as in *Diagram 30*. Make wrap wire very tight!

F.   These diagrams are shown without wrap wire covers. If you decide to use wrap wire covers, the wrap wire must be a minimum of 6" long. *See Chapter 11, page 79.*

G.   It is important to make sure that the center wire is twisted. If it isn't, the entire group of wires could slip off easily.

H.   Using a wide blade pocket knife, separate (bend) each individual wire as in *Diagram 31*.

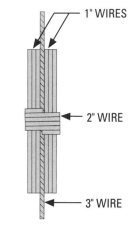

Diagram 30

Diagram 31

Diagram 32

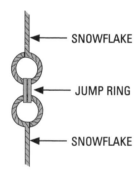

SNOWFLAKE

JUMP RING

SNOWFLAKE

Diagram 33

I. Space them as evenly as possible to make them (for effect) as symmetrical as possible.

J. Using the round nose pliers, make a loop at each end of the twisted center wire. *See Diagram 32.*

K. The snowflakes can be connected by making a jump ring with the wide part of the round nose pliers. *See Diagram 33.*

L. A good snowflake garland would be about 100 "flakes" long. Spare time (if you have any) can be occupied with making them since they are so easy to do. Individual flakes can serve a myriad of purposes! For example:

1. Decorating wrapped gifts.

2. Incorporate into other holiday decorations. (Centerpieces, wreaths, tree balls, individual tree ornaments)

3. Earrings—using **one** or **three** in tandem.

4. Short garlands over doorways.

5. Hang from light switch cords.

6. These also can be made into necklaces in many, many different formats but first they must be modified so the cut ends will not snag or catch on clothing. The modification is as follows:

M. Double the length of the 6 arms of the snowflake and follow the Steps A through K. Then bend over each of the 6 arms (at the halfway point) 180 degrees (in the opposite direction and make sure they are pressed together tightly. (Each one individually).
See Diagram 34. These rounded ends prevent snags.

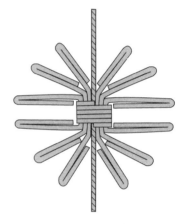

Diagram 34

**Suggested combinations of materials
for the snowflake garlands:**

1. Copper and Sterling Silver

2. Copper and Gold-filled

3. Gold-filled and Sterling Silver

4. Sterling Silver and Gold-filled and Copper

5. Brass and Copper

6. Sterling Silver and Gold-filled and Brass and Copper

7. Red, Green and Silver

8. Red, Green and Gold-filled

9. Red and Green

10. Green and Silver

11. Red and Silver

12. Green and Gold-filled

13. Red and Gold-filled

I would suggest not to mix different colored wires on individual flakes. For example:

Color combination #1:
One all copper flake followed by
one (alternating) all sterling silver flake followed by
one all copper flake, etc.

The same suggestion applies to #2 thru #13 listed on the previous page.

HAVE FUN!

CHAPTER 8

SPIRAL ICICLES
(RIBBON CANDY)

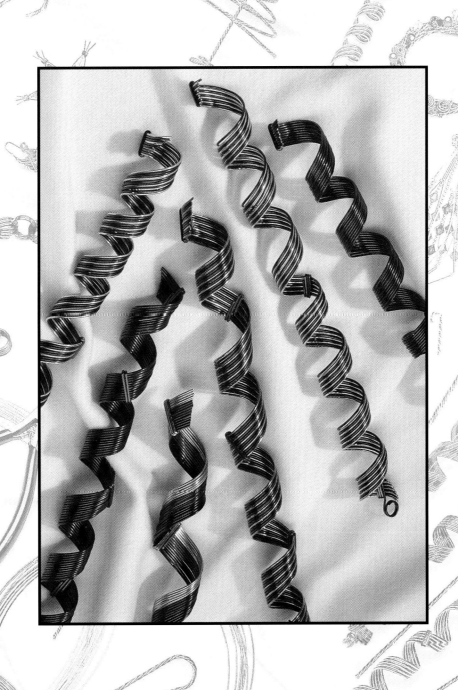

#1 SPIRAL ICICLES

This is a very popular item because of its design origin. Certain color arrangements make it look strikingly similar to the ribbon candy made years ago. You will need lots and lots of wire for these icicles and a good variety of color. I use round red/green magnet wire with brass and silver-colored craft wire. **20 GA only!**

This is a multi-wire project (up to 10 wires), and it is IMPERATIVE to use square wire to tie these wires together. DO NOT, (repeat), DO NOT use round wire to tie round wires together. It may appear to work, but round on round does not work on a permanent basis.

Most wire sources have square brass and square copper wire. I would recommend 21 or 22 GA. Square *red* and square *green* wire is nice but *it is expensive*.

This project will show you how to make a 10 wire red, green, silver spiral icicle 7 1/2" or 10" long.

> NOTE:
>
>   R = red
>   G = green
>   S = silver
>   (for color arrangement)

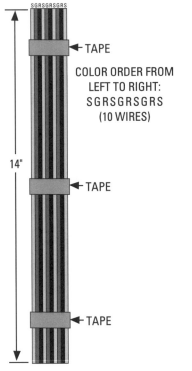

SGRSGRSGRS

←TAPE

COLOR ORDER FROM
LEFT TO RIGHT:
S G R S G R S G R S
(10 WIRES)

14"

←TAPE

←TAPE

Diagram 35

A. Cut: 4 silver round craft wires (20 GA) 7 1/2" or 15" long.

Cut: 3 red round magnet wires (20 GA) 14" long.

Cut: 3 green round magnet wires (20 GA) 14" long.

Cut: 1 square wire (21 GA) 5" long.

Cut: 2 square wires (21 GA) 3" long.

B. Arrange the round wires in the order you see in *Diagram 30* and tape them together with paper tape as indicated in *Diagram 35*.

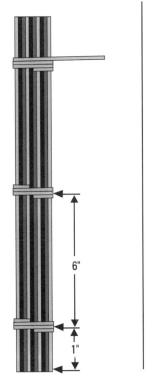

6"

1"

Diagram 36

C. Bend over the 5" square wire 1 1/2" on one end then wrap it around one end of the group of 10 wires 1" from the end of them. *See Diagram 36.*

D. When wrapping this wire around the group of 10 wires, it is IMPERATIVE that BOTH ENDS of the wrap wire end up on the SAME SIDE of the group wires.

E. Add the other wrap wires as indicated in *Diagram 36*.

F.   Remove tape. The measurements shown are not critical. The important thing is make sure the wrap wires at the ends are about 1" from the end and the center wrap is near the middle. Please note that the wrap wire ENDS are all on the SAME SIDE of the group wires. This is extremely important!

G.   Using a 1/2" dowel, proceed as follows (and using the diagrams as a guide), hold the dowel in a horizontal position and put the group wires near one end of it, making sure that the wrap wire ends are facing the dowel. See the starting position *Diagram 37*.

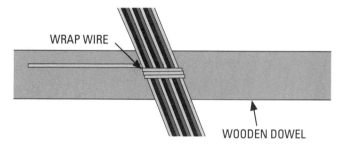

WRAP WIRE

WOODEN DOWEL

Diagram 37

H.   Pushing hard (with your left thumb over the wrap wire), grasp the group wires well below the dowel (with your right hand) and bend them across the underside of the dowel gradually moving them to the right. Keep bending them up the back side of the dowel, bringing it across the top of the dowel and to the right of your thumb which is holding down the beginning end of the group wires. This is one complete spiral turn around the dowel. You must hold down the beginning end with your left thumb while the **entire group** of wires is spiraled around the dowel. *Diagram 38*. You will quickly notice that the group wires (in the course of winding) have a tendency to roll into a twist. Simply give the **unfinished** portion a half counter clockwise turn and continue the spiral around the dowel until the icicle is **completely** spiraled around the dowel. *See Diagram 38.*

Diagram 38

Diagram 39

Diagram 40

Diagram 41

I. Before removing this icicle from the dowel, push the ends as flat as you can against the dowel, then tap them gently with the leather hammer so they conform to the overall shape of the icicle. Pull it out in a spiral motion to 7 1/2" or 3 1/2" (for the shorter one).

J. Remove the icicle from the dowel and trim the ends as indicated in *Diagram 39*.

K. Using the round nose pliers, roll the extended wrap wire into an attached jump ring. *Diagram 40*.

L. Attach a hanging hook to this. *See Diagram 41*.

M. Trim both ends as shown in *Diagram 39*. Finished icicle must be pointed at both ends.

CHAPTER 9

NAME CARD
HOLDERS

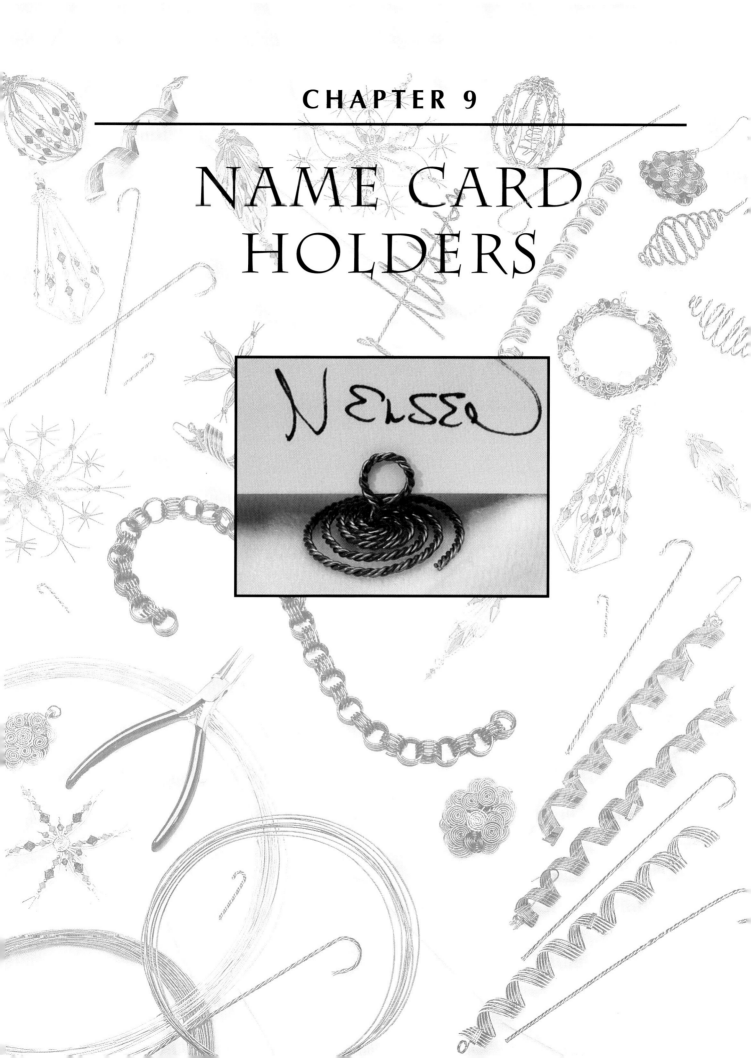

#1 NAME CARD HOLDERS

During one of my visits to Marge's home shortly before her death, we were tossing around some ideas. Two of these ideas were quickly made into prototypes. They were crude but very functional. One of them I have since refined and redesigned to be more appealing. These are the name card holders (for parties, banquets, seminars, conferences, etc.) The other idea, (napkin holders), I challenge YOU to design something unique as well as functional. Marge would be proud of you.

A.   There are two styles of name card holders: tall and short.

B.   You will need a 15" piece of wire. What type and kind is optional.

C.   For the Christmas season I recommend a 15" length of the (3) tricolored wire (green, red and silver) or (green, red, and brass) 22 GA. *See Diagram 42.*

D.   For more formal occasions, I recommend using 14 kt. gold-filled or sterling silver—you may use square only if a single wire is being used.

E.   Round wire is easier to work with. The most popular choice is 3 pieces of 22 GA (.025) round wire.

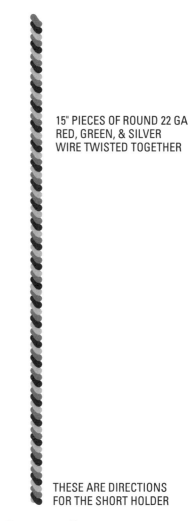

15" PIECES OF ROUND 22 GA RED, GREEN, & SILVER WIRE TWISTED TOGETHER

THESE ARE DIRECTIONS FOR THE SHORT HOLDER

Diagram 42

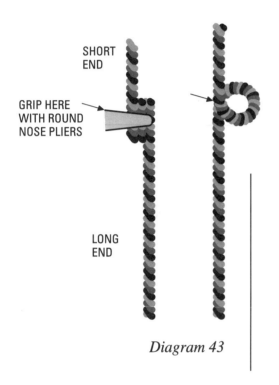

SHORT
END

GRIP HERE
WITH ROUND
NOSE PLIERS

LONG
END

Diagram 43

F.   Using the round nose pliers, grip the wire about 1"
     from one end (using the larger end of the tapered jaws)
     and wrap the wire completely around **one** jaw of the
     pliers 2 times so as to form a double loop.
     See Diagram 43.

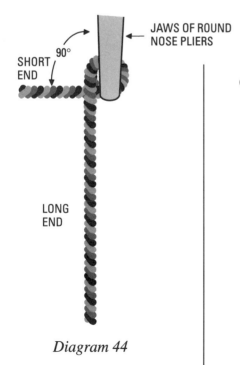

JAWS OF ROUND
NOSE PLIERS

90°

SHORT
END

LONG
END

Diagram 44

G.   Grip the wire (as indicated in *Diagram 43*) with the
     round nose pliers and bend the **short end** 90 degrees so
     that it is perpendicular to the loop. *See Diagram 44.*

H. Hold the loop in the round nose pliers so that the jaws are **parallel** to the **long end.** Bend the long wire **completely** around the short end **tightly.** Continue to wrap the long end so that it forms a flat disk at the base of the short end. Do this until all of the long end is used. While you are doing this, you will have to shift the grip of your pliers to the disk being formed as you did in Chapter 4, page 32 in making the Christmas trees. *See Diagram 45.*

Diagram 45

1. The disk now becomes platform with the loop upright and perpendicular to it. The name card is now inserted between the double wires in the loop. The loop can be tilted back just a little if you so desire. *See Diagram 45A.*

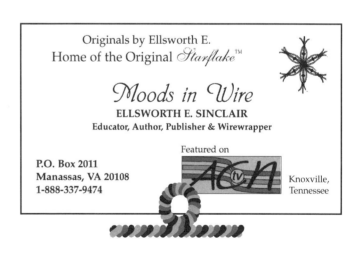

Diagram 45A

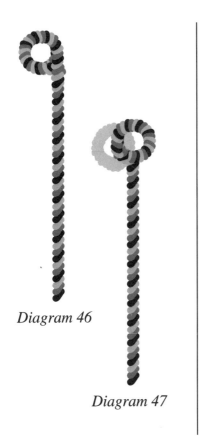

Diagram 46

Diagram 47

J.   The tall card holder is similar except the holder loop is well above the platform. This can be done as follows:

K.   Add 2" more of wire than you did in Step B previously.

L.   Repeat Step F except make the double loop **at the end** —do not leave an inch at the end. See *Diagram 46.*

M.   Using the chain nose pliers, bend back the loop (clockwise) so it is perpendicular to the rest of the wire. *See Diagram 47.*

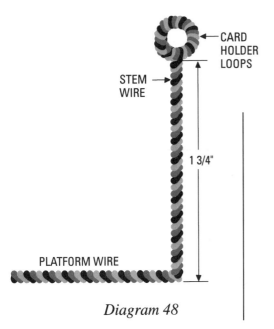

CARD HOLDER LOOPS

STEM WIRE

1 3/4"

PLATFORM WIRE

Diagram 48

N.   It's a matter of choice just how far you want the card holder loop above the platform. I prefer 1 3/4".

O.   Measure 1 3/4" from the bottom of the card holder loop and put a 90 degree bend in the wire. *See Diagram 48.*

P.   Using the round nose pliers, grip the bottom of the stem as indicated in *Diagram 49*.

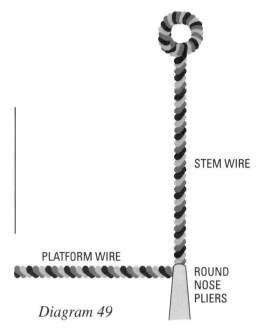

Diagram 49

Q.   Bend the platform wire around the top jaw of the round nose pliers and down the other side. Remove the pliers and immediately put them back in the loop with the bottom jaw where the top jaw was and continue to circle the base of the stem wire. This is the beginning of the platform. Continue making the flat disk (hold with the flat nose pliers) until all the wire is used.

R.   The finished tall card holder should look like *Diagram 50*.

Diagram 50

CHRISTMAS TREE CARD HOLDERS–YES!!!

S.   Same except put loop at the top of the tree.

Tree Card Holder

CHAPTER 10

LARGE BIRDCAGE TREE ORNAMENT

#1 LARGE BIRDCAGE TREE ORNAMENT

Materials:

Tricolored: 3 wire–red, green, silver, or
Bicolored: 4 wire–2 green, 2 red.

A.   Cut the wire 36" long and bend over 3" of one end 90 degrees so that it is at right angles to the rest of the wire. Bend over the other end 1" likewise in the opposite direction so you now have a giant Z. *See Diagram 51.*

B.   Using round nose pliers, grip (with the small end of the tapered jaws) the 1" wire at the base as indicated in *Diagram 52.*

C.   Bring the 32" wire across the top jaw of the pliers in the opposite direction.

D.   Bend the 32" wire around the top jaw of the pliers and down the other side. Remove the pliers and immediately put them back in the loop with the bottom jaw where the top jaw was and continue to circle the base of the 1" wire. Continue making the flat disk holding it with the wide nose (flat nose) pliers until approximately 1/2 of the wire is used. *See Diagram 53.*

E.   Repeat this process from the opposite direction. *Diagram 54.*

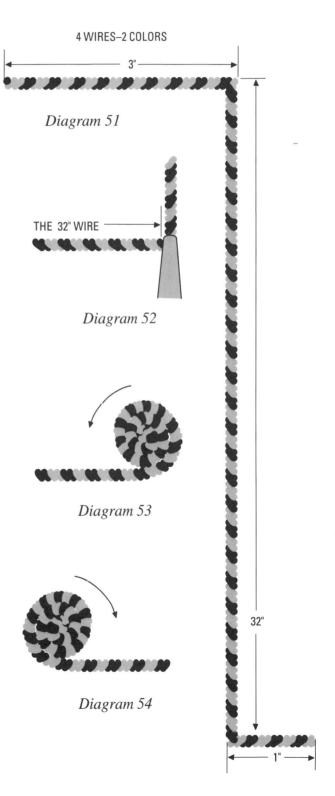

4 WIRES–2 COLORS

3"

Diagram 51

THE 32" WIRE →

Diagram 52

Diagram 53

Diagram 54

32"

1"

73

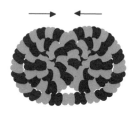

Diagram 55

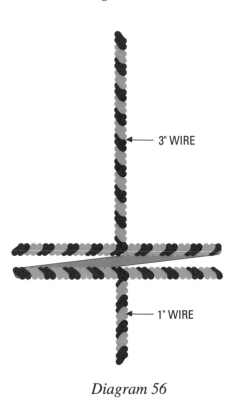

← 3" WIRE

← 1" WIRE

Diagram 56

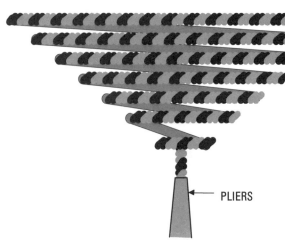

← PLIERS

Diagram 57

F.   Now you have two flat disks of wire being rolled toward each other. *See Diagram 53.* Keep rolling them (alternately) until all the wire is used but you now have one disk on top of the other with the center wires pointed in opposite directions. *See Diagrams 55 and 56.* Make sure the disks are as close to the same size as possible.

G.   Both of these disks have a "stem" sticking out of the center and each is perpendicular to it and pointing in the opposite direction. These disks must be pulled out with these "stems" in order to form a large oval-shaped birdcage tree ornament.

H.   Proceed, very carefully, as follows: Hold the assembly (*Diagram 56*) in your left hand and using the flat nose pliers, grasp the 1" stem and while holding the assembly with the fingers covering all but the center of the bottom half. Tug firmly (but gently!) 1/4" until the first coil of the bottom part of the assembly is out about 1/4" from the rest of the coils. *See Diagram 57.*

74

CHAPTER 10   LARGE BIRDCAGE TREE ORNAMENT

I. Move the fingers of the left hand back slightly to release the second coil of the disk—pull again with the pliers-firmly, (but gently). Repeat this process until the bottom half is completed. *See Diagram 58.*

J. Turn over the entire assembly and repeat Steps H and I with the other half.

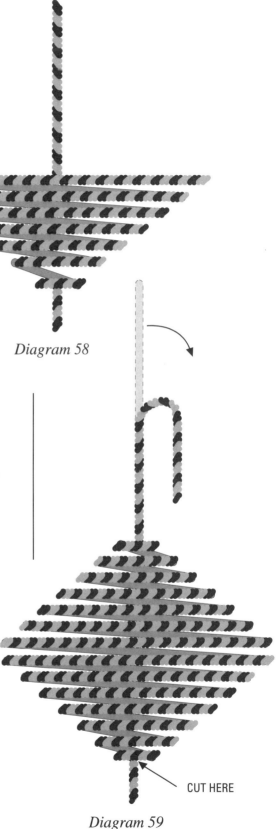

Diagram 58

K. It is important to note that when you pull out the coils of this cage, the symmetry is not as even as shown by the diagram. By PRACTICE and manipulation of these coils, you can get them to look very close to the ideal shape as seen in *Diagram 59.*

L. The short stem at the bottom can now be cut off as close to the first coil as possible.

M. The long stem at the top is to be made into a hook for hanging on the tree. Proceed as follows: Using the round nose pliers (large part of the jaws) bend as indicated in *Diagram 59.*

CUT HERE

Diagram 59

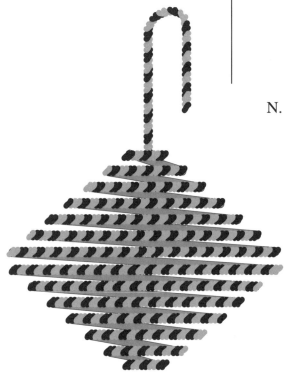

N.   See completed ornament in *Diagram 60*.

**FINISHED BI-COLORED (4 WIRE)
BIRDCAGE TREE ORNAMENT**

Diagram 60

WRAP WIRE
COVER

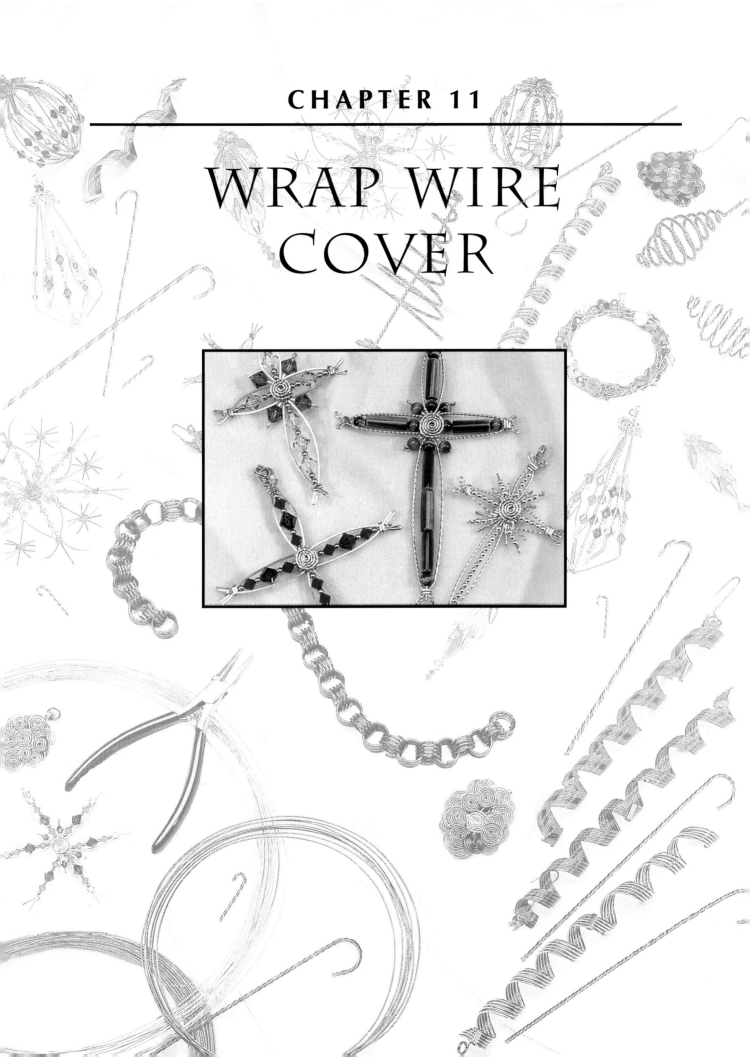

#1 HOW TO MAKE A WRAP WIRE COVER

As a wirewrapper, I am constantly experimenting, refining and practicing old and new techniques. From this daily routine I am constantly coming up with new ideas, new designs, and now, new innovations. To share these with you is one of the prime goals of Volume III.

After a couple of hours into my daily routine of practice wrapping, I was trying to develop a way to hide bare wrap wires and still incorporate these into the design of the piece being wrapped. It wasn't long before that inner glow of excitement began to lead me to the threshold of this new concept. In just a matter of minutes, I knew this idea would fulfill the criteria of being functional and aesthetically pleasing to any design into which it may be incorporated. It is my pleasure to share this with you.

A.   Practice with 21 GA (.028) square brass practice wire.

B.   Cut 9 wires 5" long.
      Cut 1 wire 8 1/2" long and bend it over in the middle (4 1/4" mark) 180 degrees. *See Diagram 61.*

C.   Tape the 9 wires together at one end—make sure they are flat and even. *Diagram 62.*

D.   Put the wrap wire on the group wires as shown in *Diagram 63.*

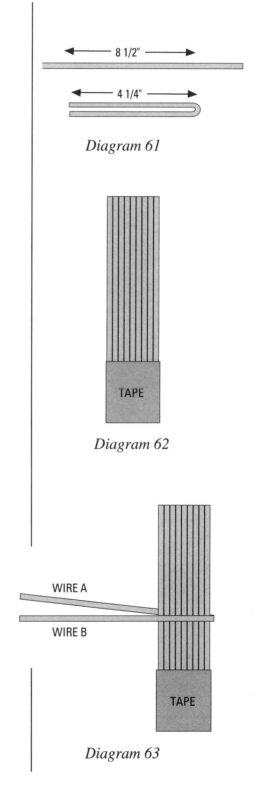

Diagram 61

Diagram 62

Diagram 63

E. Wrap the wire around the group wires in equal amounts until you have near equal amounts left (from Wire A and Wire B). *See Diagram 64.*

F. It is **imperative** to note this pattern: Wire A and Wire B point in the same direction, but please note that Wire B is underneath the group wires and Wire A is not.

G. Bend Wire A down 90 degrees so that it is perpendicular to the group wires.

H. Bend Wire B up 90 degrees so that it is perpendicular to the group wires.

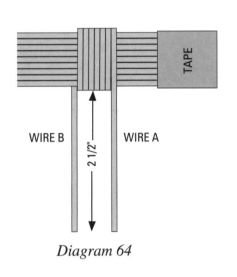

Diagram 64

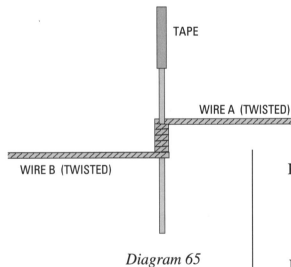

Diagram 65

I. *Diagram 65* shows the group wires standing on end with the edge facing you. Check what you have done against this diagram.

J. Using the pin vise, put a fine twist on the full length of Wire A and Wire B.

K. Using the round nose pliers (small end), make a loop in
    the end of Wire B. *See Diagram 66.*
    Roll this loop tightly along itself (Wire B).
    It will become a flat wire disk.

    Using the wide nose pliers to hold it flat, roll it
    clockwise so the edge of the disk finally over-
    laps the wrap of the group wires 1/8".

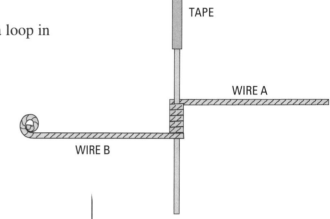

Diagram 66

After this is done, then bend the disk 90 degrees so it is
flat up against and covering the group wires on one side.
See Diagrams 67 and 67A.

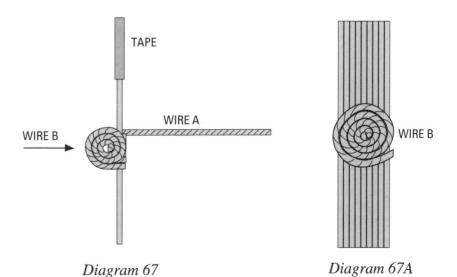

Diagram 67   *Diagram 67A*

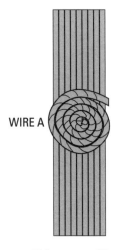

WIRE A

Diagram 68

Diagram 69

L.   Repeat this process for Wire A. *See Diagram 68.*

M.   Finished wrap wire cover should show a flat twisted wire disk covering the wrapped wire on either side of the group wires. *See Diagram 69.*

N.   Save this entire assembly for future use in Chapter 14, page 101 covering basic Starflakes.

O.   This wrap wire cover can be used extensively where bare wrap wires need to or want to be covered. Do not use this innovation on men's rings.

P.   There is a variation of this wrap wire cover which can be used on the 3-dimensional tree balls. This involves a wrap wire cover with a 4" right angle center post. Refer to Chapter 12, page 85.

CHAPTER 12

WRAP WIRE
COVER WITH
CENTER POST

CHAPTER 12   WRAP WIRE COVER WITH CENTER POST

#1 WRAP WIRE COVER WITH CENTER POST

This wrap wire cover with a 4 1/2" to 5" center post is used exclusively for the round, teardrop, and square tree ball. Please keep in mind that a center post is *not required* for tree balls, but the center post sure does add a lot to its looks. It forces the focus of the eye to see more sharply the depth of the ball, rather than having your vision go through it.

There are other "things" that can be put in the center of these tree balls. These "Items" will be suggested in another chapter.

A.   Follow the directions beginning in Chapter 11, page 79 .

Changes:

1. Cut 9 wires 10" long.

2. Cut 1 wire 13 1/2" long.

3. Bend this longer wire over so one end is 4 1/4" to 4 1/2" long and the other length is 8 1/4" to 8 1/2" long. *See Diagram 70.*

B.   Wrap Wire A and B around the ten group wires as shown in *Diagram 71*. Measurements of Wire B are not critical—just keep in mind that enough wire is needed to make the wrap wire cover (2 1/2") plus 4 1/2" to leave for the center post and hook holder.

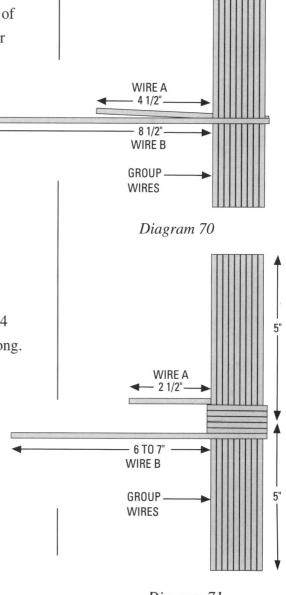

WIRE A
4 1/2"

8 1/2"
WIRE B

GROUP
WIRES

Diagram 70

WIRE A
2 1/2"

6 TO 7"
WIRE B

GROUP
WIRES

5"

5"

Diagram 71

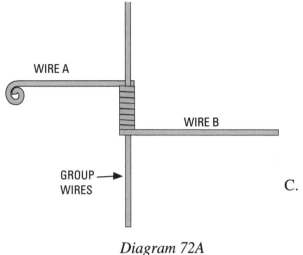

WIRE A

WIRE B

GROUP
WIRES

Diagram 72A

C.   See Steps F, G, H, and J in the previous chapter
     except Wire A is shorter than Wire B.

D.   Roll Wire A into a flat disk and fold over as in
     Chapter 11, page 82.

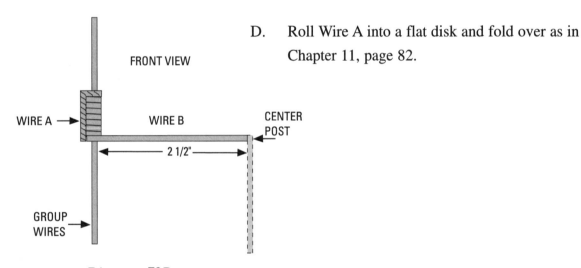

FRONT VIEW

WIRE A

WIRE B

CENTER
POST

2 1/2"

GROUP
WIRES

Diagram 72B

E.   On Wire B measure out 2 1/2" and bend the wire
     90 degrees up toward your face. Proceed to wrap
     Wire B around the base of the center post. *See
     Diagrams 71 and 72*, as you did when making the tall
     card holder.

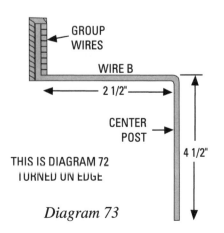

GROUP
WIRES

WIRE B

2 1/2"

CENTER
POST

4 1/2"

THIS IS DIAGRAM 72
TURNED ON EDGE

Diagram 73

CHAPTER 12   WRAP WIRE COVER WITH CENTER POST

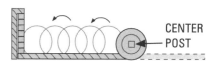

Diagram 74

F.   It would be helpful if you would take some
     practice wire (brass or copper) and run through
     this procedure several times to work out any
     unexpected problems you may encounter. The
     diagrams are clear, but they can be "confusing"
     if you are not familiar with the procedure.

Diagram 75

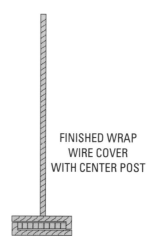

Diagram 76

ANGELS

#1 ANGELS

These angels are another example of experimentation with variations of a previous system. In Volume II, *Moods in Brass & Glass,* there is a section on how to make cages—pages 71-86. This is the same system that is used to make angels except for two major changes which are: Using longer wires and bending these longer wires differently!

The angels illustrated in this chapter are an average size (6" wires will make a 2 1/2" tall angel). If you want it taller, use 8" or 10" wires. Smaller ones can be made with 4" wires. These smaller angels can be mounted inside of a wire tree ball—see Chapter 19, page 153, Diagram 174.

A.　Cut 6 wires, 22 GA square 8" long.

B.　Cut 2 wires, 22 GA square 3" long.

C.　Bend one of the 3" wires in half.

D.　Bend the other 3" wire over 1/2" on one end.

E.　Put the six 8" wires together and tape the ends as in *Diagram 77*.

F.　Using the 3" wire that is bent over 1/2" on the end, wrap it around the group wires as shown in *Diagrams 78A and 78B* **exactly**. Do not cut off the longer wire yet, but cut off the excess of the shorter end so that it does not overlap beyond the group wires.

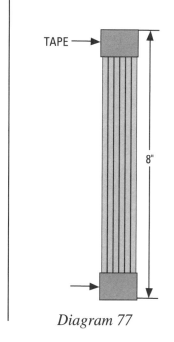

TAPE

8"

Diagram 77

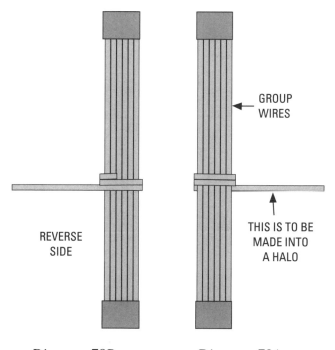

GROUP WIRES

REVERSE SIDE

THIS IS TO BE MADE INTO A HALO

Diagram 78B　　*Diagram 78A*

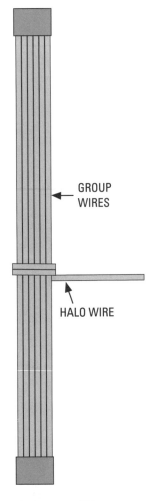

Diagram 79

G.   Using size **one** on the ring mandrel, wrap the halo wire (*Diagram 79*) around the mandrel completely so that the circle (halo) is no more than 1/4" away from the group wires. *See Diagram 80.*

It is **very important** that the other end of the halo wire be on the inside (out of sight). *Diagram 79* shows the correct position to begin bending the halo. For this halo to be effective, the wire must remain as flat as possible. Do not even put the slightest twist into it.

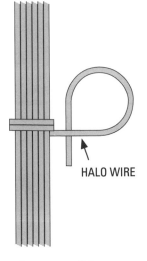

Diagram 80

H.   Bend it in a complete circle (shape is more important than size). Just be sure it is not too large for the angel.

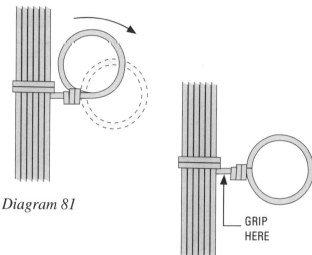

Diagram 81

I. Proceed to *Diagrams 81 and 82*. They are self-explanatory. Cut off excessive wire.

J. Using the round nose pliers, grip the halo stem as indicated in *Diagram 82* and bend up and over so the round halo is centered directly over the wrap wires. *See Diagram 83*.

Diagram 82

K. As you continue working on this angel, please be extremely aware of the finished halo. It can take a beating if you are careless or forgetful.

L. Put the assembly flat on a ruler and place the wrap wires (and halo) over the exact center of the group wires— *See Diagram 84* and mark 3/4" out on each side of the center.

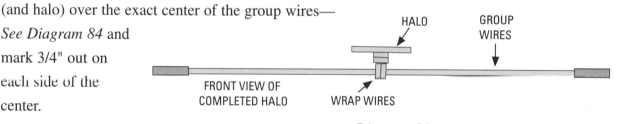

Diagram 83

M. Using the wide nose pliers, bend up the group wires at each 3/4" mark. Make sure you bend them up together, one side at a time. Bend up about 30 degrees. *See Diagram 85*.

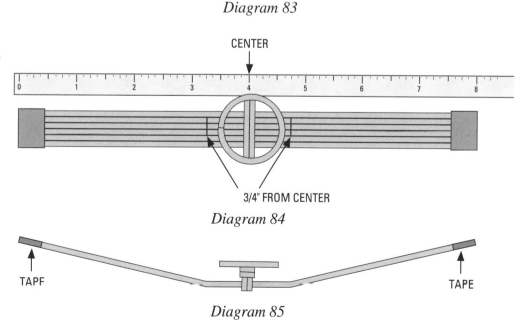

Diagram 84

Diagram 85

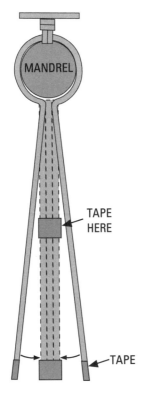

TAPE
HERE

TAPE

Diagram 86

WRAP WIRE

ALL TAPE
REMOVED

Diagram 87

N.   Using a ring mandrel, place the assembly directly over the 1 1/2" size mark. Carefully push down the group wires on either side of the halo. It will not go quite all the way around but try to touch the group wires directly underneath where the halo is.
See Diagram 86.

O.   As you remove the assembly from the mandrel, it will not be as round as shown in the diagram. It will be more oval (which more closely resembles the shape of the human face).

P.   To make things easier, squeeze the group wires together and put a piece of tape around them as indicated in *Diagram 86*.

FROM THIS POINT ON, THE HALO WILL NOT BE INCLUDED IN EVERY DIAGRAM.

Q.   Using the other 3" wire that has been bent in half, wrap it around the two sets of group wires so that they are permanently tied together. *See Diagram 87.*
Make sure that the ends of this wrap wire **are facing toward the back of the halo**.

R.   There are 6 group wires on each side of the angel. The distance from the halo to the tip of the group wires should be approximately 4".

S.   With the **back** of the halo facing you, bend up the first 2 wires together on each set of group wires. *See Diagram 88.*

T.   Using the round nose pliers, grip the two wires at the same place and bend as indicated on each side of the head. *See Diagram 89.*

U.   Using two pair of wide nose pliers, twist the ends of the wing wire together. Make sure there is at least 1/8" between the holding pliers and the twisting pliers. Twist slowly and gently **3 times** and cut off any excess wire as in *Diagram 91.*

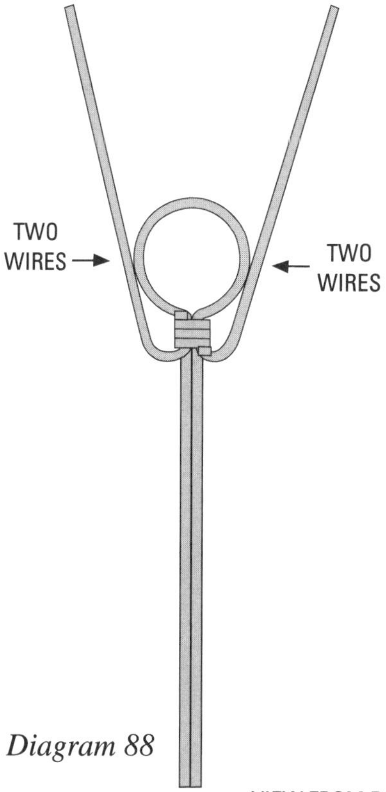

TWO WIRES →   ← TWO WIRES

Diagram 88

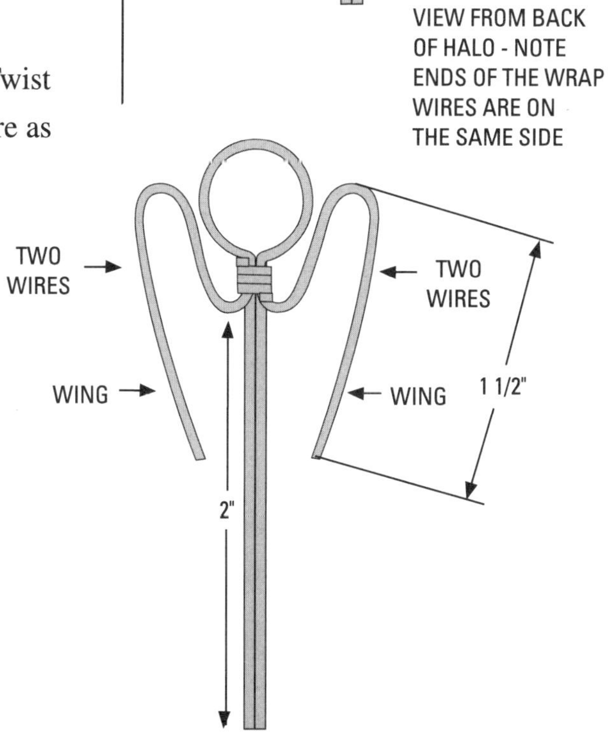

VIEW FROM BACK OF HALO - NOTE ENDS OF THE WRAP WIRES ARE ON THE SAME SIDE

TWO WIRES →   ← TWO WIRES

WING →   ← WING   1 1/2"

2"

Diagram 89

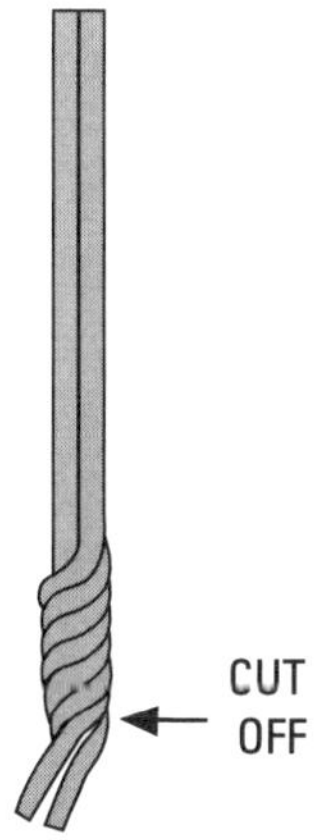

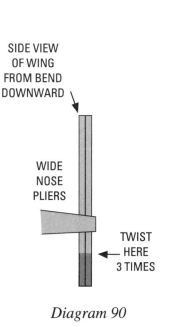

SIDE VIEW OF WING FROM BEND DOWNWARD

WIDE NOSE PLIERS

TWIST HERE 3 TIMES

CUT OFF

Diagram 91   *Diagram 90*

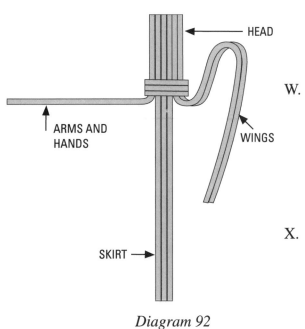

Diagram 92

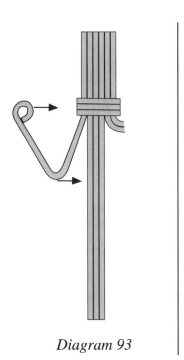

Diagram 93

V. Using the wide blade of the knife, spread the two wing wires apart on each wing. This gives them a 3-D look and adds to their depth. (See photo, page 89)

W. On the opposite side of the assembly (from where you turned up the wires for the wings), turn up one wire from each group so that it is perpendicular to the rest of the group wires. *See Diagram 92.* These are the arm wires.

X. Measure out 1/2" from the group wires and bend both arm wires up more than 90 degrees with the round nose pliers. This bend is the "elbow" so how far you bend it depends on how and where you want to position the arms. It is suggested to put the arms and hands in a praying position, so you can bend accordingly.

Just remember, always make the bends in each arm together so you can ensure balance and accuracy. When you have completed the bends in *Diagram 93*, then spread the arms at the elbows and manipulate the wires into a more accurate praying position with the wide nose pliers. After spreading the elbows, you will have to push (gently!) down on the hands to lower the elbows. The most ideal position would be for the praying hands to be about level with the wrap wire or slightly lower. Check *Diagram 93* and also the photos.

Y.   The remainder of this project is the easiest part. There
     are **6** remaining group wires (3 on either side). Put them
     (or hold them) together and trim the ends so that they
     are the **same length.** This is VERY IMPORTANT!

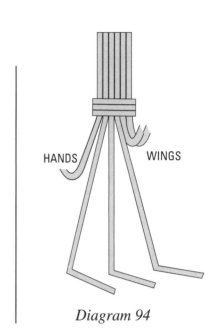

Diagram 94

Z.   Measure 3/4" from the end of **each wire** and mark it.
     When each wire is marked, then spread them apart and
     bend each one (at the mark) 90 degrees to the right. *See
     Diagram 94.* Make sure each wire is bent 90 degrees to
     the right. (All 6 wires.)

Proceed as Follows:

1. Beginning with any wire, make a small hook on
   the end of each 1/2 flange. *See Diagram 95* (bottom view). Put hook "B" around group Wire "C",
   and with the chain nose pliers, squeeze it gently
   so it is firmly secured.

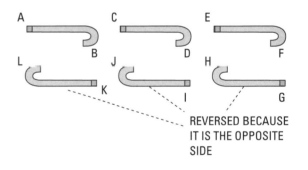

   Do likewise with   D to E
                        F to G
                        H to I
                        J to K
                        L to A.

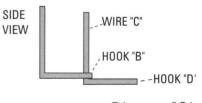

Diagram 95A

2. You should now have a segmented interlocking rec-
   tangle at the base of the angel. It can stand on its
   own but it is not stable.

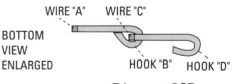

Diagram 95B

BASE OF ANGEL BEFORE

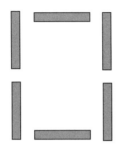

Diagram 96A

BASE OF ANGEL AFTER

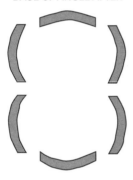

Diagram 96B

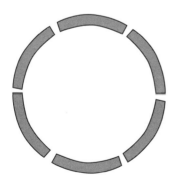

Diagram 96C

3. To stabilize it, do the following: Using the medium part of round nose pliers, grip **each segment** firmly one at a time and push the ends toward the center of the angel. This will, in effect, make the "skirt" of the angel round and add the necessary stability. It may require tightening some connections.

4. This base should be as circular as possible for stability. *Diagram 96C*

NINE WIRE STARFLAKES

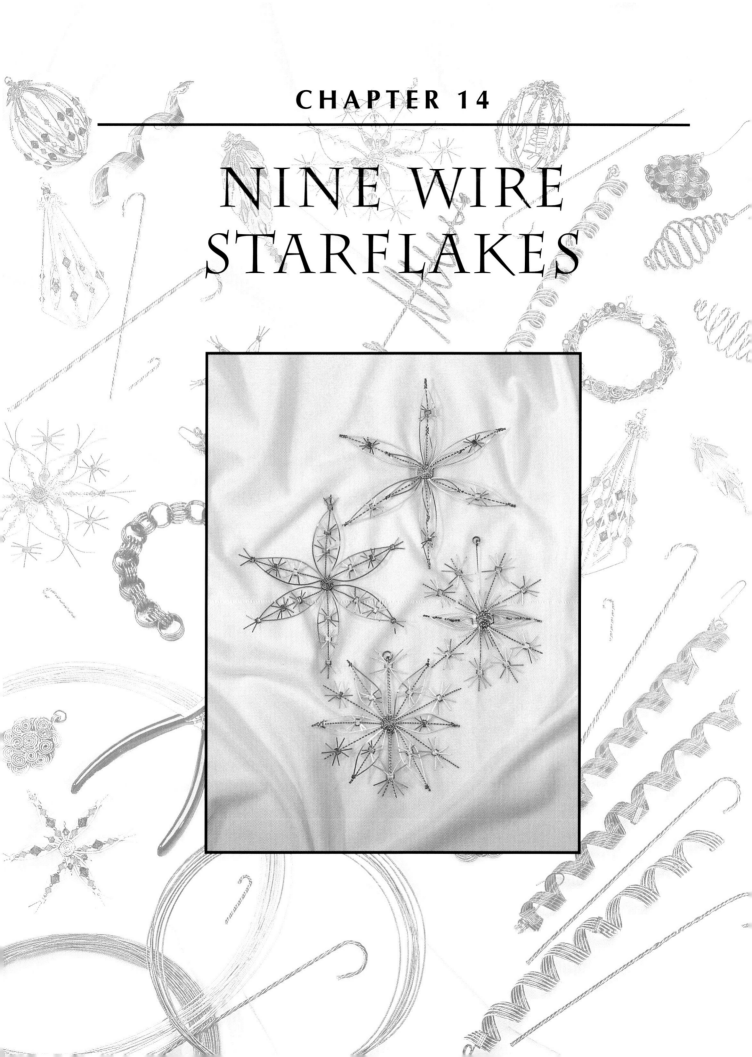

CHAPTER 14   NINE WIRE STARFLAKES™

#1 STARFLAKES—NINE WIRE

Without a doubt, the starflake is one of the most unique of all these innovative wire decorations (except the tree balls). Of course its versatility is beyond measure.

This chapter will cover instructions only for 9 wire. The other variations will be shown in completed drawings. There will also be all wire starflakes shown.

A.   Cut 8 wires 4" long, 22 GA, Square

Cut 1 wire 5" long, 22 GA, Square

Cut 6 wires 1 1/2" long, 22 GA, Square

Cut 1 wire 8" long, 22 GA, Square

Clean and straighten all wires with the jewelers cloth.

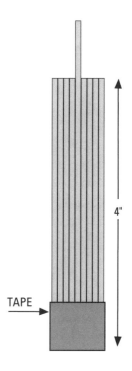

Diagram 97

B.   Bend over one end of the 1 1/2" wires 1/2" (180 degrees).   Bend over the 8" wire 180 degrees at the halfway point. This is going to be the wrap wire and the cover for it. See Chapter 11, pages 79–82.

C.   Put the nine wires together, with the 5" wire in the center, so that they are flat at each end. Put tape around one end (*Diagram 97*) to hold them in place while you use the folded 8" wire to wrap them securely and make the cover. *See Diagram 98.*

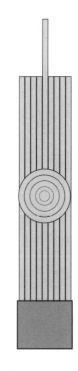

Diagram 98

101

CHAPTER 14 NINE WIRE STARFLAKES

ENLARGED FOR DETAIL

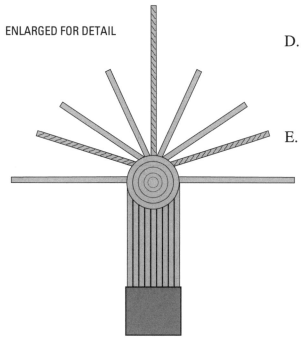

Diagram 99

D.   Separate the wires that are not taped into groups of 3 as in *Diagram 99* and with the pin vise, twist the center wire of each group.

E.   There are a variety of options (see below) available to you now. You can elect to put any number of beads on the twisted wires: choose any size (2mm to 6mm) or any color in any format. A few suggestions are shown below. *See Multi-Diagram 100 (A,B,C).*

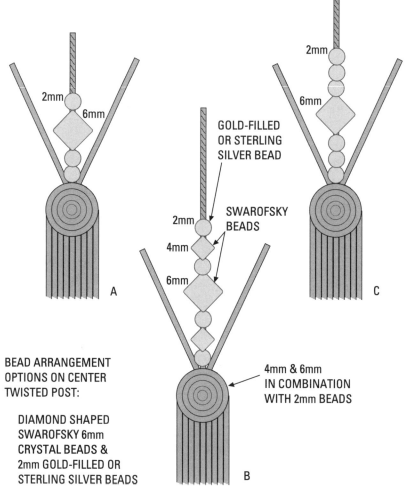

OTHER OPTIONS
1. ALL 2mm BEADS
2. ALL 4mm CRYSTAL BEADS
3. DIFFERENT COMBINATIONS OF EACH

BEAD ARRANGEMENT OPTIONS ON CENTER TWISTED POST:

DIAMOND SHAPED SWAROFSKY 6mm CRYSTAL BEADS & 2mm GOLD-FILLED OR STERLING SILVER BEADS

GOLD-FILLED OR STERLING SILVER BEAD

SWAROFSKY BEADS

4mm & 6mm IN COMBINATION WITH 2mm BEADS

Multi-Diagram 100

CHAPTER 14   NINE WIRE STARFLAKES

F. When you have finished putting the beads on the center twisted wire, then the other two wires in the group must frame the beads. Using your thumb and forefinger pushing in the opposite directions, you can form a long arc on either side of the wire with the beads on it. They can be tied where the three wires come together. *See Diagrams 101, 102, and 103.* Use the flat nose pliers to bend as indicated. Tie these together using the six 1 1/2" wires already cut and bent.

Diagram 101

Diagram 102

G. The center wire is 1" longer than the rest of the wires. This extra length is to be used to make a loop so the starflake can be hung by putting a jump ring through it and attach it to a hand-made hook. *See Diagram 104.*

Diagram 103

Diagram 104

H. After the other 2 groups of wires are done in the same way, remove the tape and separate the wires into 3 groups of wire as you just did for the top half.

I. When you have all 6 groups completed (with beads and tie down), spread them evenly so they look like a 6 "arm" star.

J. Decision time again! If you just want to hang this on your tree (or in the window as a sun catcher), all you have to do is cut off the ends 1/4" out from the wrap wire. (Do not cut off the hanging wire!)

K. The other twisted center wires can be cut off just barely beyond the wrap wire.

L. If you want to wear this as a pendant, then first cut off (flush) the twisted center wires on the ends, EXCEPT the HANGING wire. Cut off the other wires and leave them long enough to bend over double to eliminate the jagged ends which can snag on clothing.
See Diagram 105.

Diagram 105

CHAPTER 15

ELEVEN WIRE STARFLAKES

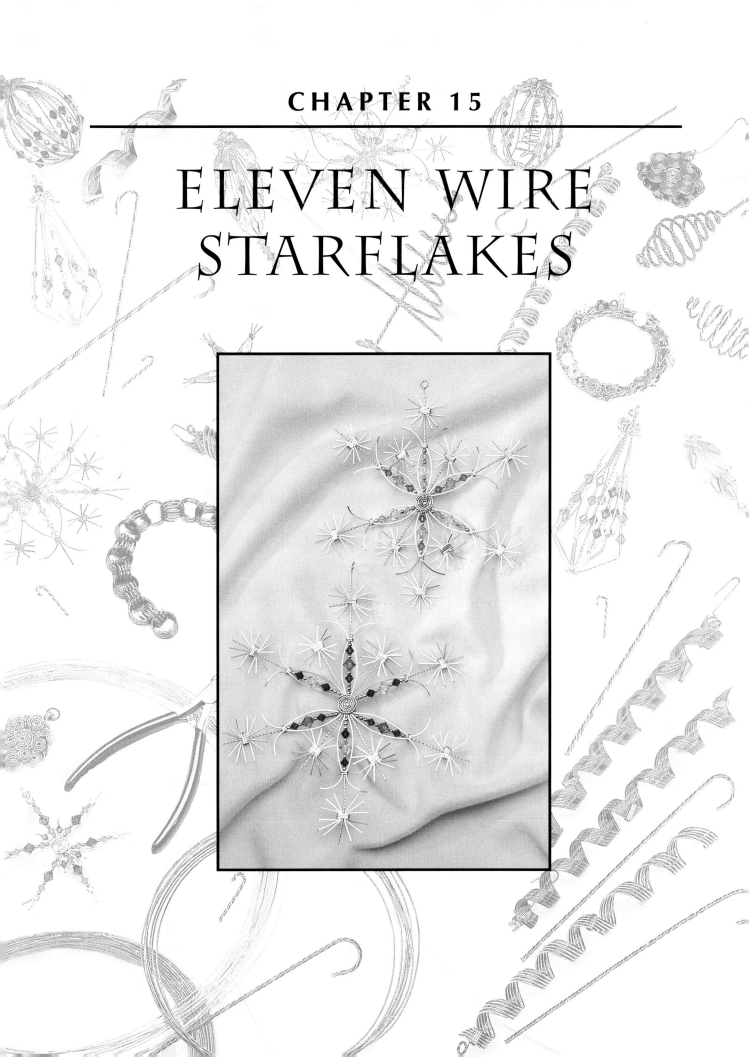

#1 ELEVEN WIRE STARFLAKE

A GOOD COMBINATION IS:

    STERLING SILVER—9 WIRES WITH
    2mm SILVER BEADS AND
    6mm COBALT BLUE SWAROFSKY
    CRYSTAL BEADS

    ADDED WIRES WITH
    SNOWFLAKES IN COPPER WIRE

HOOK END ASSEMBLY
FOR **ALL** STARFLAKES

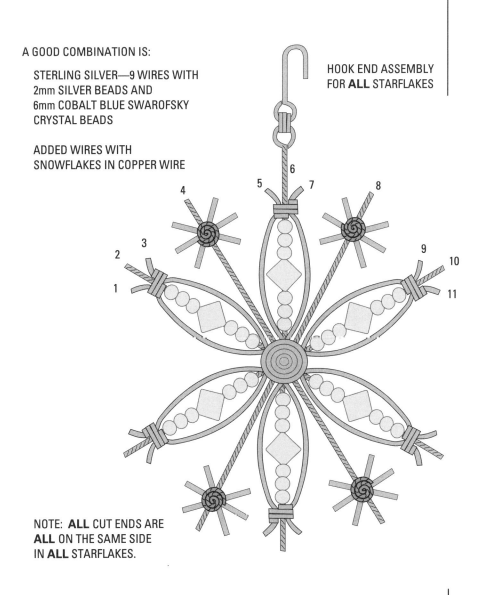

A "SNOWFLAKE" CAN
BE ADDED TO EACH OF
THESE EXTRA WIRES.

SEE *Diagram 31,* CHAPTER 7
PAGE 53 FOR MORE
ACCURATE BENDING AND
PLACEMENT OF WIRES.

NOTE: **ALL** CUT ENDS ARE
ALL ON THE SAME SIDE
IN **ALL** STARFLAKES.

Diagram 106

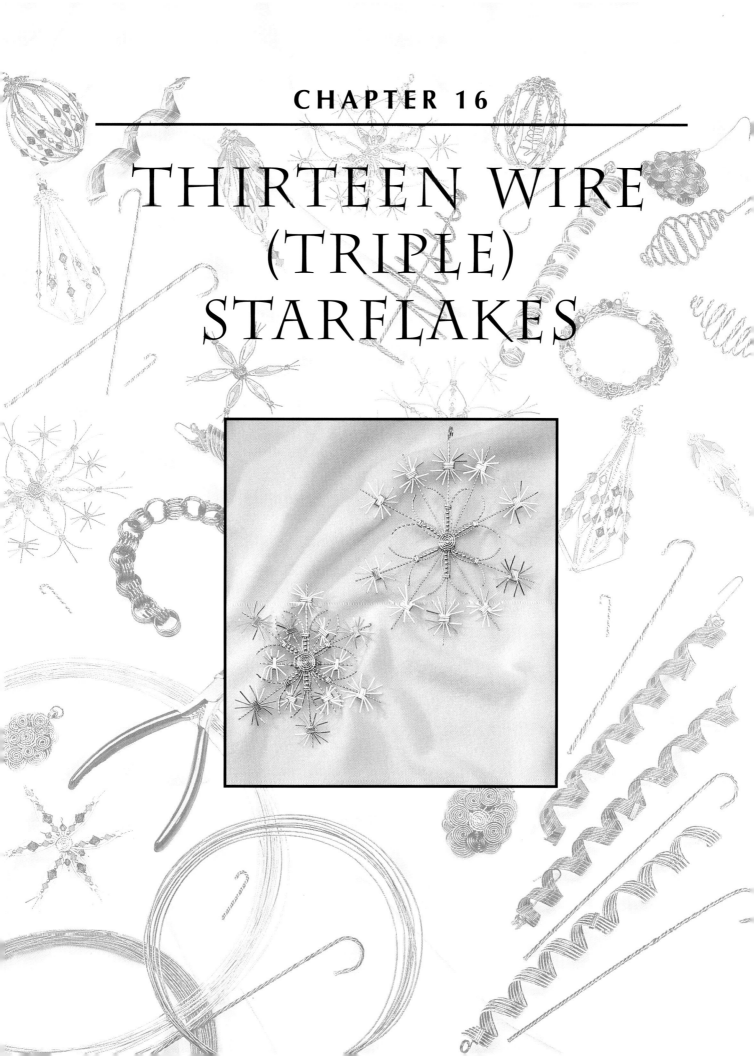

CHAPTER 16

THIRTEEN WIRE (TRIPLE) STARFLAKES

#1 TRIPLE STARFLAKES

Level #1

Additional horizontal wires are added as in *Diagram 107*.
Once the additional wires are tied together, then the different
levels of the starflake can be put together. Project should resemble *Diagram 107A* below which shows **Level #1** completed.
(See following page for instructions on beading and tying wires.)

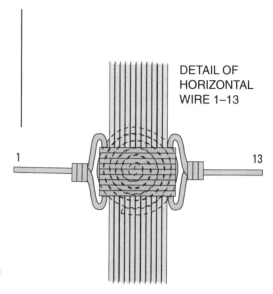

DETAIL OF
HORIZONTAL
WIRE 1–13

Diagram 107

A GOOD COMBINATION IS:

STERLING SILVER—9 WIRES WITH
2mm SILVER BEADS AND
6mm COBALT BLUE SWAROFSKY
CRYSTAL BEADS

ADDED WIRES WITH
SNOWFLAKES IN COPPER WIRE

HOOK END ASSEMBLY
FOR **ALL** STARFLAKES

A "SNOWFLAKE" CAN
BE ADDED TO EACH OF
THESE EXTRA WIRES.

SEE *Diagram 31*, CHAPTER 7
PAGE 53 FOR MORE
ACCURATE BENDING AND
PLACEMENT OF WIRES.

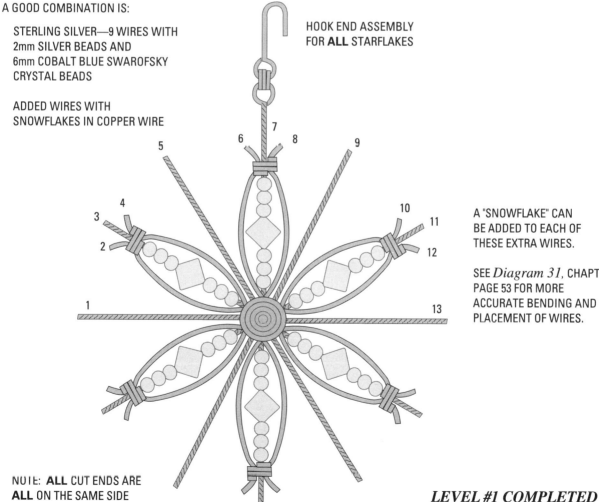

NOTE: **ALL** CUT ENDS ARE
ALL ON THE SAME SIDE
IN **ALL** STARFLAKES.

LEVEL #1 COMPLETED

Diagram 107A

CHAPTER 16   THIRTEEN WIRE (TRIPLE) STARFLAKES™

Each arm (#3 #7 #11) in *Diagram 107A* contains, alternately
three 2mm sterling silver beads,
one 6mm crystal bead.
Then 3 more 2mm sterling silver beads.

A. Put beads on wire #3, then tie together wires #2, #3, #4, as seen in *Diagrams 100 thru 104*.
Cut off only excessive wrap wire.

B. Repeat this same process for wires #6, #7, #8.

C. Repeat this same process for wires #10, #11, #12.

D. Repeat this same process for wires #14, #15, #16.

E. Repeat this same process for wires #18, #19, #20.

F. Repeat this same process for wires #22, #23, #24.

#2 LARGER MIDDLE WIDER STAR

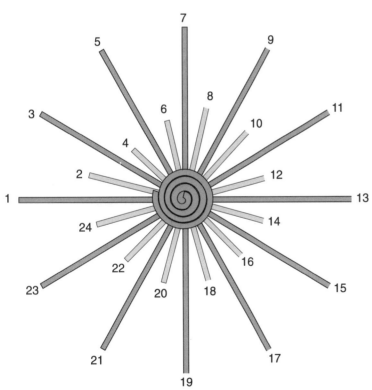

13 WIRE TRIPLE STARFLAKE: ENLARGED DIAGRAM GUIDE FOR DIRECTIONS A THRU G, PAGE 112-113 & A THRU C PAGE 113

Diagram 109

Level #2

Wires #1, #5, #9, #13, #17, #21—
Each contains in this order (*See Diagram 109A,* page 114) Five 2mm beads, one 6mm crystal bead, one 2mm bead, one 6mm crystal bead, one 2mm bead, one 6mm crystal bead, one 2 mm bead. (11 beads total)

A. Put beads on wire #1, then using one of the 2" tie wires, tie together (as seen in *Diagrams 100 to 104*) wires #24, #1, #2. Cut off only excessive wrap wire.

B. Put the same arrangement of beads on wire #5; then using one of the 2" wrap wires, tie together wires #4, #5, and #6 as in *Diagrams 100-104*.

112

C.   Put the same arrangement of beads on wire #9; then using one of the 2" wrap wires, tie together wires #8, #9, #10 as in *Diagrams 100 101*.

D.   Likewise with wire #13 and #12, #13, #14.

E.   Likewise with #17 and #16, #17, #18.

F.   Likewise with wire #21 and #20, #21, #22.

G.   #24, #1 and #2 should be done.

CAUTION: #24, **#1**, #2/#12 , **#13**, #14 should be kept as horizontal as possible to keep the symmetry. Numbers 1 and 13 wires are the most important!

Level #3

A.   Put a "Snowflake" on (near the end) of wires #3, #7, #11, #15, #19, and #23. *See Diagram 31,* page 53.

B.   There are many different patterns and arrangements of beads in this triple starflake. Also with longer wires, the pattern could progress to a level 4 or 5. **Be bold! Experiment!!**

C.   Make sure the #7 wire is long enough to accommodate the snowflake as well as the hanging hook.

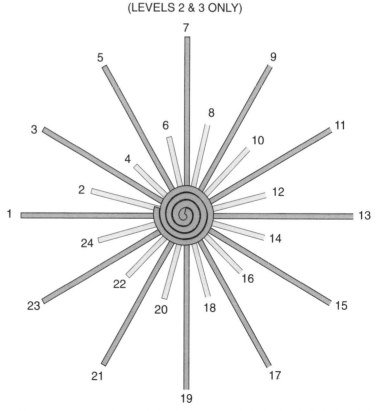

(LEVELS 2 & 3 ONLY)

13 WIRE TRIPLE STARFLAKE. ENLARGED DIAGRAM GUIDE FOR DIRECTIONS A THRU G, PAGE 112-113 & A THRU C PAGE 113

Diagram 108

FINISHED TRIPLE STARFLAKE SHOWING
NUMBERED WIRES IN FINAL TIEDOWN,
MINI-SNOWFLAKES AND HOOK.

Diagram 109A

NOTE: ALL **CUT** ENDS ARE ON THE **SAME** SIDE

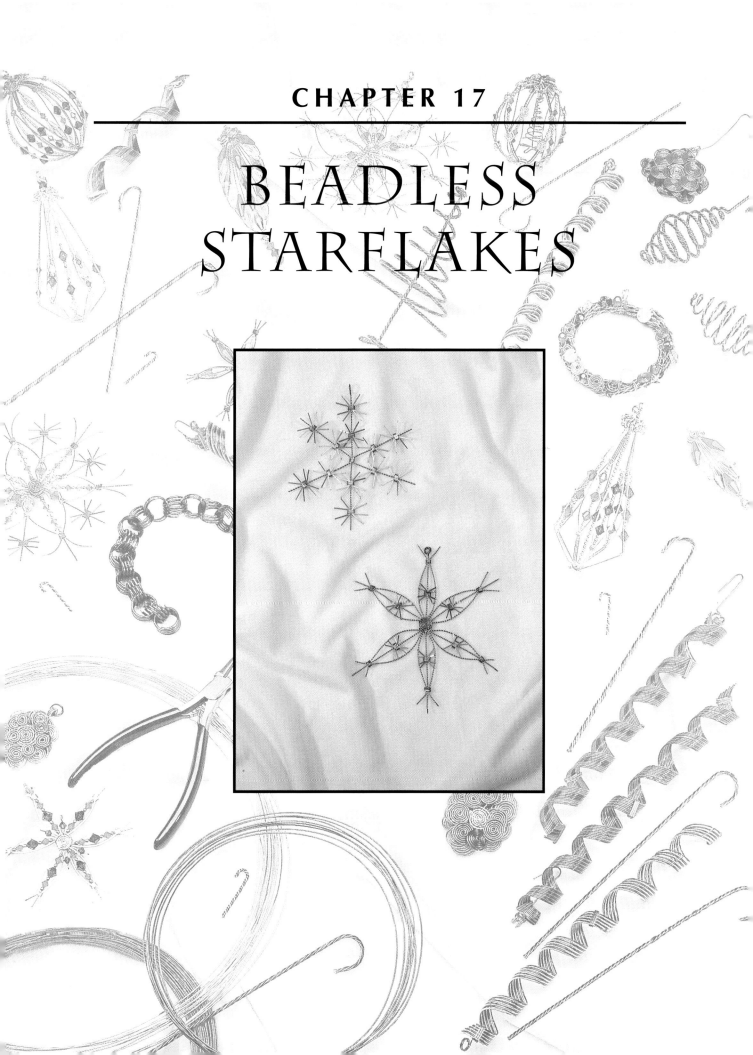

BEADLESS
STARFLAKES

#1 THREE WIRE SIMPLE STARFLAKE

After you have developed a satisfactory comfort level making these large starflakes, the next several pages are designed to offer suggestions of the infinite possibilities that lie ahead. They cover everything from beginning with 3 wires up to 20 wires. The minimum length of wires should be at least 4". I would encourage you to begin with the simple designs first. None of these suggested designs is complicated as long as you proceed step by step (one at a time) until it all comes together. Relax and have fun!!

Options:

      1. All gold-filled wire.

      2. All sterling silver wire.

      3. Gold star with silver flakes.

      4. Silver star with gold flakes.

Refer to *Diagrams 30 and 31, page 53* for making
      the "Flakes." Either 4 or 6 wires is acceptable.

COULD BE USED AS A TREE ORNAMENT
      OR AN EARRING.

Diagram 110

117

#2 THREE WIRE WITH DOUBLE FLAKES

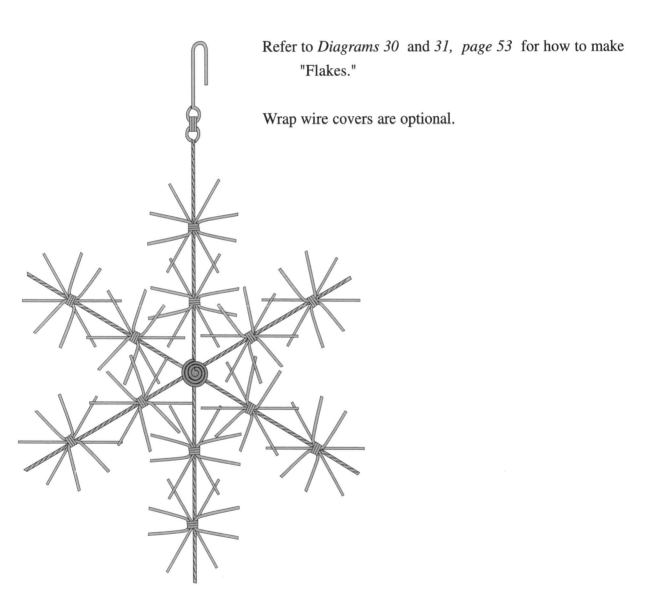

Refer to *Diagrams 30* and *31, page 53* for how to make "Flakes."

Wrap wire covers are optional.

Diagram 111

#3 NINE WIRE SIMPLE ORNAMENT/ EARRING

Most effective when made with a mixture of plain/ twisted/ gold/ silver wire.

A.   Tie all 9 wires together with an 8" wrap wire. (Wire for the wrap AND the wrap wire cover)

B.   For making a wrap wire cover refer to *Diagrams 61 thru 68, pages 79-82.*

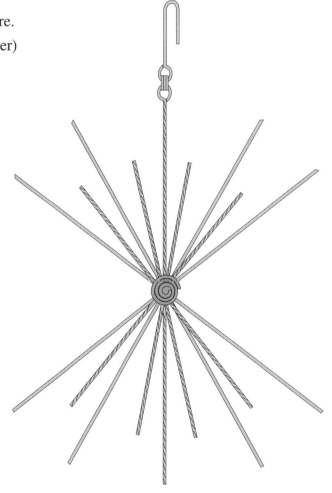

Diagram 112

#4 SIMPLE NINE WIRE STARFLAKE

Simple Nine Wire Starflake with no wrap wires
(except for center wrap wire and cover)

A.   Follow *Diagrams 97, 98,* and *99.*

B.   To the center twisted wire of each group of three, add
2 or 3 1" wires as seen in *Diagram 31, page 53.*

THIS IS NOT SUITABLE
FOR WEARING.

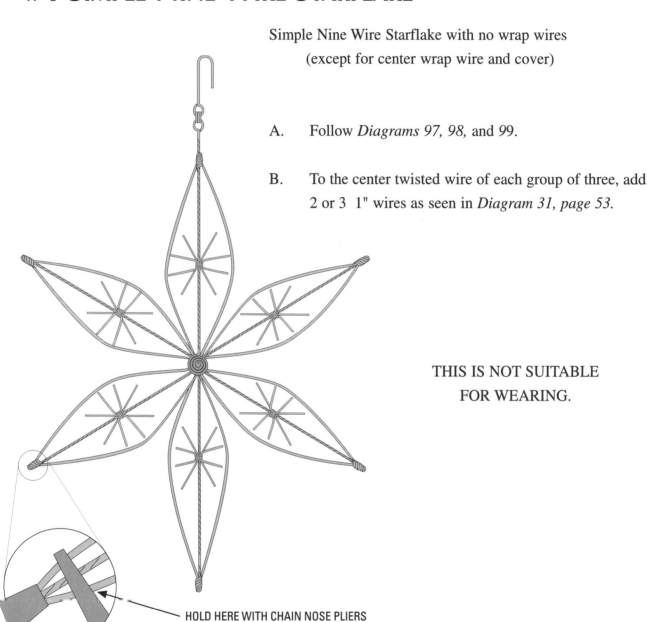

HOLD HERE WITH CHAIN NOSE PLIERS

TWIST WITH **FLAT NOSE** PLIERS THREE **1/2 TURNS.**
MAKE SURE THE FLAT NOSE PLIERS ARE AT LEAST 1/8" FROM
THE CHAIN NOSE PLIERS BEFORE YOU BEGIN TWISTING.
(ANY CLOSER AND THE WIRES COULD BREAK)

Diagram 113

#5 SIMPLE NINE WIRE STARFLAKE

Simple Nine Wire Starflake with conventional wrap wires.

A.   Wrap wire covers are optional.

B.   All wires are twisted.

THIS IS NOT FOR WEARING UNLESS
    MODIFIED AS IN *Diagram 34.*

Diagram 114

#6 A SMALLER TRIPLE STARFLAKE

NOT SUITABLE FOR WEARING
    UNLESS MODIFIED.

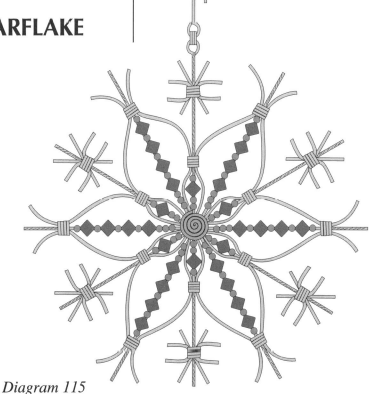

Diagram 115

#7 DOUBLE STARFLAKE WITH ADDED SNOWFLAKES

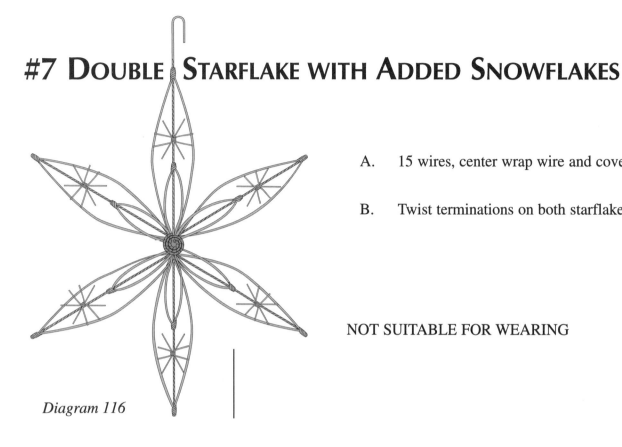

A.   15 wires, center wrap wire and cover

B.   Twist terminations on both starflakes.

NOT SUITABLE FOR WEARING

Diagram 116

#8 THE "APOSTLE" STARFLAKE

A.   One center wrap wire and cover

B.   Twist terminations

C.   "12" Snowflakes.

NOT SUITABLE FOR WEARING

Diagram 117

#9 ALL TWISTED WIRE DOUBLE FLAKE STARFLAKE

A.   Center wirewrap cover

B.   Conventional terminations

C.   Could use wrap wire covers
     where indicated

NOT SUITABLE FOR WEARING.

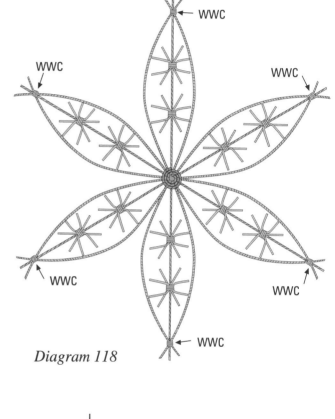

Diagram 118

#9A WIRE NOT TWISTED

Same as above only not all wire is twisted

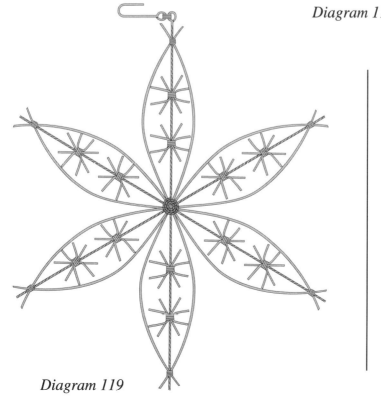

Diagram 119

#10 THE NOVA

A. Top: hanging wire

B. Bottom: 20 / 21

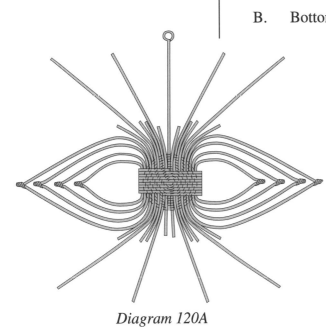

Diagram 120A

SUPER NOVA

Diagram 120B

C. Wrap wire covers can be added.

#11 BEAD ARRANGEMENT
OPTION A

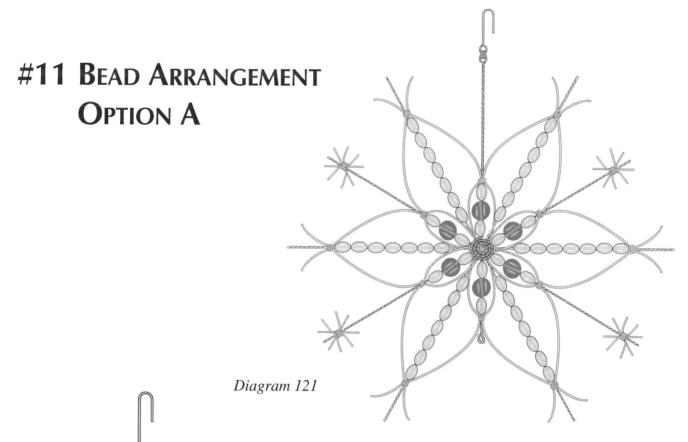

Diagram 121

#12 BEAD ARRANGEMENT OPTION B

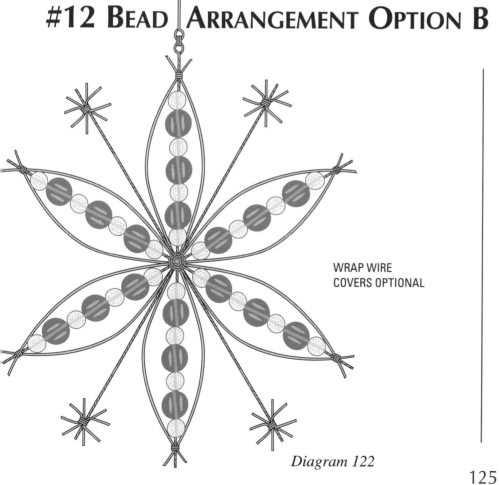

WRAP WIRE
COVERS OPTIONAL

Diagram 122

#13 NORDIC MOTIF

Diagram 123

A.   Wrap wire covers are optional.

CHAPTER 18

CROSSES

#1 CROSSES

Crosses are a very popular item with a wide variety of design. A large percentage of my crosses are made with the diamond-shaped Swarofsky (Austrian crystal) beads (6mm and 4mm). Mineral beads, square, rectangular, round, or tubular-shaped can also be used.

The basic design for the cross involves using 5 wires; however, there is an optional 7 wire design which will be included in this chapter. There will also be, at the end of this chapter, suggestions as to the infinite variety of bead pattern arrangements. It is important to note at this time that *you should have a large stock of 2mm (drilled) gold-filled/ sterling silver beads.* They are a very integral part of the design for these crosses (and starflakes). *In every case, one or two 2mm beads always separates a crystal or mineral bead from the next one*. For further clarification, refer to the color pictures in this book.

It is also important to note at this time that you will be instructed to cut the wires longer than necessary. When you become comfortable with the concept, then you can cut the wire shorter.

5 Wire Cross:

A.   Cut 5 wires (22 GA square) 4" long.
       Cut 2 wires (22 GA square) 6" long.
       Cut 4 wires (22 GA square) 2" long.

                Always clean and straighten the wire
                   before starting on every project!!!

B.   You will need:
        6 4mm drilled Swarofsky beads.
       12 2mm drilled gold-filled beads.

1. If you are doing the optional 7 wire design, then you will need additional material:

   2 additional 2" wires (22 GA square)

   4 additional Swarofsky beads

   8 additional 2 mm drilled gold-filled beads

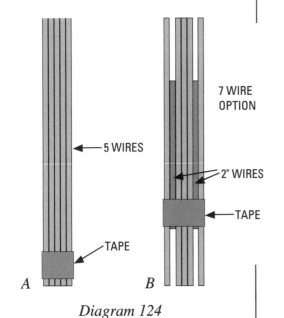

Diagram 124

C.   After you have cleaned and straightened the wire, then:

1. Bend over (180 degrees) 2" of each end of the 6" wires.

2. Bend over (180 degrees) 1/2" of 4 (or 6) of the 2" wires.

D.   Arrange the 5 wires as shown in *Diagrams 124A* and *124B*.

E.   Measure 2 1/4" from the top of the 5 wires and mark. If you are doing the 7 wire option, do the same, except make sure that each of the 2" wires has an equal amount of wire above and below the finished wrap. *See Diagram 124B.*

F. The 2" section of this wrap wire (in this case) becomes the left side cross section of the cross— continue to wrap the longer part of this wire around the group of 5 wires **three** times. *See Diagrams 125A and B and 126.*

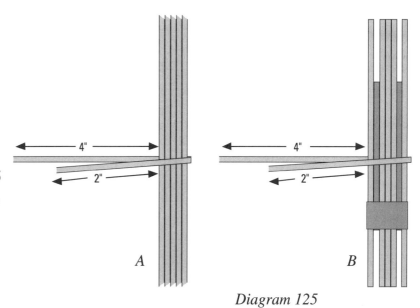

Diagram 125

G. The 7 wire is done exactly the same. Make sure the 2" wires do not slip.

H. With the second 6" wire, do the same thing only in the opposite direction and make only 2 1/2 turns around the group wires with the cover wire. *See Diagram 127 for clarity.* IT IS ACCURATE! The 7 wire is done the same way.

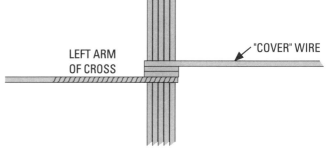

Diagram 126

7 Wire Cross:

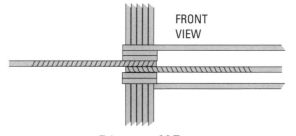

Diagram 127

I. Twist the shorter (cross arms) wires as shown in *Diagram 127*.

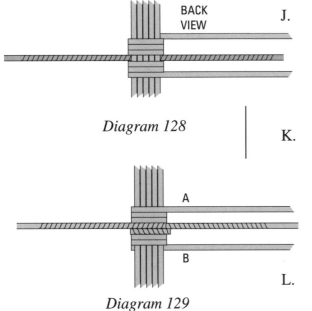

Diagram 128

Diagram 129

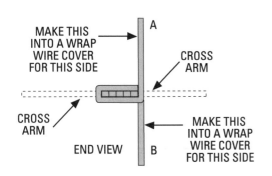

Diagram 130

J. The cross arms wires are, obviously, not on the same level (one is above or below the other).

K. There is a procedure by which the eye can be fooled into thinking they are really opposite each other on the same level (since the wrap wire cover will hide this little deception!) *See Diagram 129.*

L. Looking at the front view and using the wide nose pliers, grip the right cross arm about 1/8" from the group wires and bend it up about 60 degrees, then again gripping it about 1/8 inch beyond the bend you just made, bend it down again until it is just about horizontal. *See Diagram 129.* When this is done properly, the wrap wire cover will hide it.

M. Next: Bend Wires A and B like you are going to wrap them around the group wires again, but this time only bend them 90 degrees so that they are in opposite direction from each other and perpendicular to the entire assembly (in opposite directions). *See Diagram 130.*

N. Twist Wires A and B and cut them so they are 2 5/16" long.

O. Follow the instructions for making wrap wire covers in Chapter 11, pages 79-82.

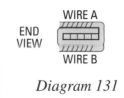

WIRE A
END VIEW
WIRE B

Diagram 131

P.   The finished wrap wire cover should look like *Diagram 131*.

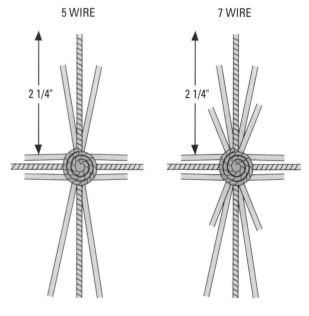

5 WIRE   7 WIRE

2 1/4"   2 1/4"

Diagram 132A   *Diagram 132B*

Q.   Remove tape from group wires and spread the wires as indicated. The outside wires are bent down to form the rest of the horizontal arms. *See Diagram 132A and B.*

R.   Twist the center wire (top and bottom section).

S.   Put two 2mm gold-filled beads on the center wire (top section) followed by a 4 mm diamond-shaped Austrian crystal bead, then followed by one 2mm gold-filled bead. *See Diagram 133.*

T.   Holding the assembly in the right hand, bend (shape) the other 2 wires in the group with the thumb and forefinger of the left hand (if you are left-handed, use the opposite hands!) as indicated in *Diagram 133*. Tie down with 2" wire.

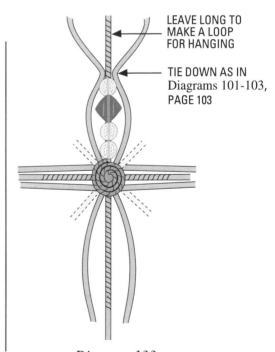

LEAVE LONG TO MAKE A LOOP FOR HANGING

TIE DOWN AS IN Diagrams 101-103, PAGE 103

Diagram 133

133

U. Repeat this process for the horizontal arms except put only one bead on each side of the 4mm crystal bead. DO NOT CUT OFF EXCESS WIRE YET!

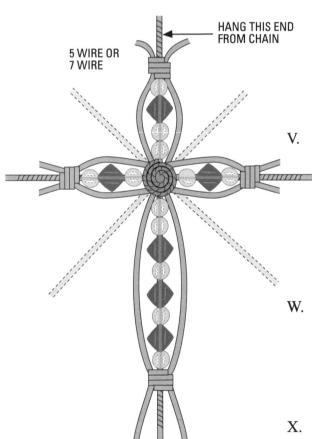

HANG THIS END
FROM CHAIN

5 WIRE OR
7 WIRE

Diagram 134

V. On the bottom section of the cross, put (in this order) from the center out: Two 2mm gold-filled beads, one 4mm crystal bead, one 2mm gold-filled bead, one 4mm crystal bead, one 2mm gold-filled bead, one 4mm crystal bead, one 2mm gold-filled bead. *See Diagram 134.*

W. Put a round loop in the center top wire—how much you curl it depends on how long you want it to dangle from the chain. Consult *Diagram 104, page 103* in this book. (The added jump ring is not necessary.)

X. The rest of the wires can be clipped off and bent over double as in *Diagram 34, page 55* in this book. They should be no more than 1/4" long **after bending**. They must be bent over. This eliminates the rough end which can snag clothing!

Y.   If you are doing the 7 wire, proceed as follows for each of the 4 wires (2 top, 2 bottom):

1. On each wire put a 4mm crystal bead on it with a 2mm bead on either side of it. *See Diagram 135A.*

2. Cut the wire 1/8" to 3/16" on the end away from the center of the cross.

3. Bend this double with the smallest end of the round nose pliers. This prevents the beads from coming off. See color illustrations for finished project. *See Diagram 135B.*

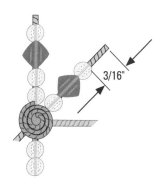

Diagram 135A

SIDE VIEW
Diagram 135B

Z.   Crosses to put on (or at the top) of your Christmas tree or as part of your holiday decorations need to be large to be seen. (The smaller ones have a tendency to get lost if thcy arc not worn on a chain around thc ncck.) To makc the large ones, think not only about cutting longer wire, but a good guideline is 3 to 1 for the beads. If there is one bead on top, then there should be ONE bead on each horizontal part and THREE beads on the bottom vertical part. Likewise 2, 2, 2 and 6/ or 3, 3, 3 and 9.

The most popular cross I make is:

Twisted Gold wire with 2, 2, 2, and 6 bead arrangement using all 2mm sterling silver beads.

Drawing it does not do it justice!

There are suggestions on the pages that follow for varying bead arrangements.

5 WIRE
4mm BEADS
2, 2, 2, 6

Diagram 136

7 WIRE,
6mm BEADS
1, 1, 1, 3 (5 WIRES)
1, 1, 1, 1 (2 WIRES)

Diagram 137

CROSS SUGGESTIONS

5 WIRE
4mm BEADS
1, 1, 1, 3

Diagram 138

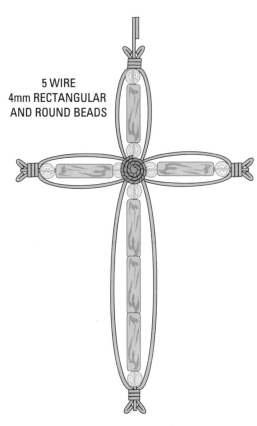

5 WIRE
4mm RECTANGULAR
AND ROUND BEADS

Diagram 139

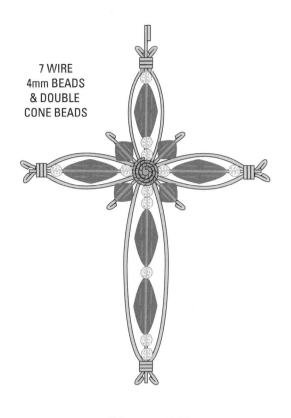

7 WIRE
4mm BEADS
& DOUBLE
CONE BEADS

Diagram 140

7 WIRE,
RECTANGULAR &
OVAL BEADS

Diagram 141

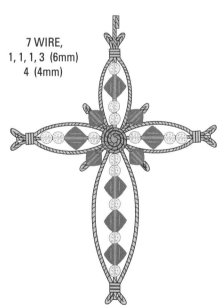

7 WIRE,
1, 1, 1, 3 (6mm)
4 (4mm)

Diagram 142

137

5 WIRE,
6mm ROUND BEADS
3, 3, 3, 9

Diagram 143

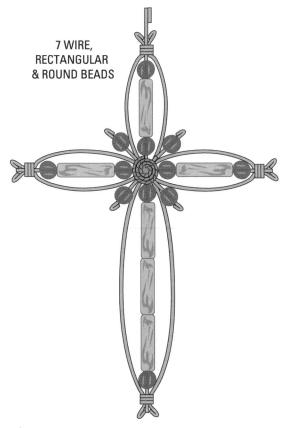

7 WIRE,
RECTANGULAR
& ROUND BEADS

Diagram 144

7 WIRE,
CLEAR CRYSTAL
DOUBLE CONE BEADS
WITH 4mm BEADS

Diagram 145

5 WIRE,
RECTANGULAR
& ROUND BEADS

Diagram 146

138

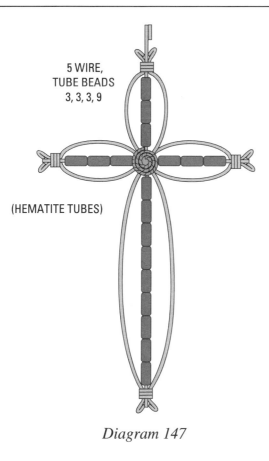

5 WIRE,
TUBE BEADS
3, 3, 3, 9

(HEMATITE TUBES)

Diagram 147

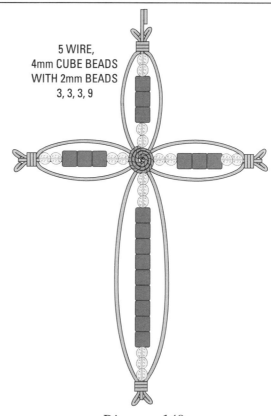

5 WIRE,
4mm CUBE BEADS
WITH 2mm BEADS
3, 3, 3, 9

Diagram 148

5 WIRE,
RECTANGULAR
& ROUND BEADS
1, 1, 1. 3

Diagram 149

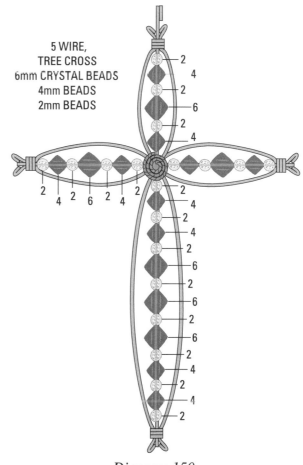

5 WIRE,
TREE CROSS
6mm CRYSTAL BEADS
4mm BEADS
2mm BEADS

Diagram 150

CHRISTMAS TREE BALLS

#1 TEARDROP, ROUND AND SQUARE

Before beginning any projects in this chapter, please, (please!) go back and reread the introduction at least twice. Think about what is written. Also do not begin any projects in this chapter if you are not an experienced wirewrapper! Do not think of these projects as complicated!! They are not! Just do one simple step at a time!

A.   The number of beads used may vary. It all depends on what format (style) is being followed, or what size bead is being used.

There are three basic shapes. Only the round has a slight variation, which will be shown on another page.

B.   For any tree ball (of any shape) always use nine 22 GA square wires **10" long**.

Supplement these wires with:

   1 22 GA square wire 13 1/2" long

   6/12 22 GA square wire 2" long.
      (Bend over 1/2" of one end of these.)

   1 22 GA square wire 8" long, twisted

C.   Put the 9 wires 10" long together so they are flat and even. Tape one end tightly.

Other variations will be shown on another page.
Also look at the color photos.

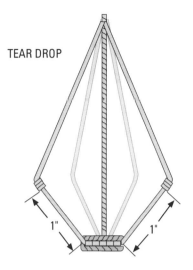

TEAR DROP

1"   1"

Diagram 151

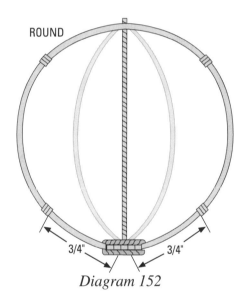

ROUND

3/4"   3/4"

Diagram 152

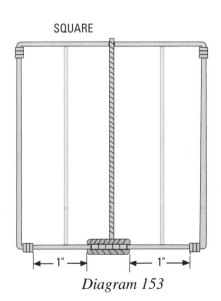

SQUARE

1"   1"

Diagram 153

CHAPTER 19 CHRISTMAS TREE BALLS

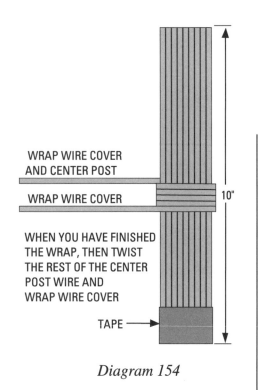

WRAP WIRE COVER
AND CENTER POST

WRAP WIRE COVER

WHEN YOU HAVE FINISHED
THE WRAP, THEN TWIST
THE REST OF THE CENTER
POST WIRE AND
WRAP WIRE COVER

TAPE

10"

Diagram 154

D. Using the 13 1/2" length already cut, bend over one end of it 5 1/2" 180 degrees. This wire will serve as a wrap wire and cover (5 1/2") and on the other end (8"), it will be part wrap wire, part wrap wire cover and also a center post for the Christmas ball. For this wrap wire, cover, and center post, follow the instructions in Chapters 11 and 12, pages 79-87, in this book.

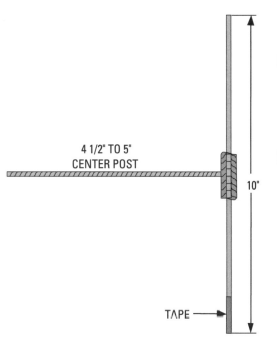

4 1/2" TO 5"
CENTER POST

10"

TAPE

Diagram 155

E. If you have followed directions properly, your assembly should look like *Diagram 155*.

F. Make sure, as you continue this project, that the center post wire is always pointed up.

G.   Leave the tape on (for now) and begin to separate the group of nine wires (above the wrap wire cover) into 3 groups of 3. *See Diagram 156.*

H.   Twist the center wire of each group of 3. *Diagram 156* This prevents slippage through the wrap wire.

I.   Unlike the smaller starflake in Chapter 14 (*Diagrams 100-103*), you have 2 choices at this point: Which format do you want to follow? These choices are shown in *Diagrams 157 and 158.* These are the 2 styles of tree balls mentioned earlier.

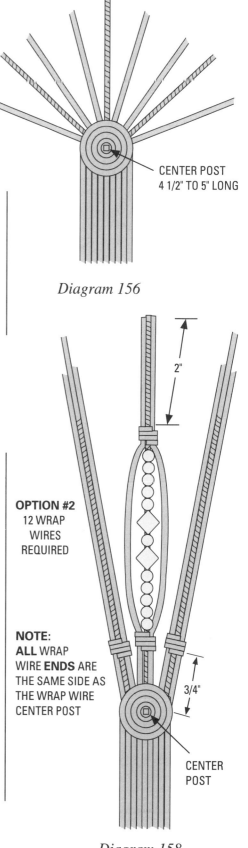

CENTER POST
4 1/2" TO 5" LONG

Diagram 156

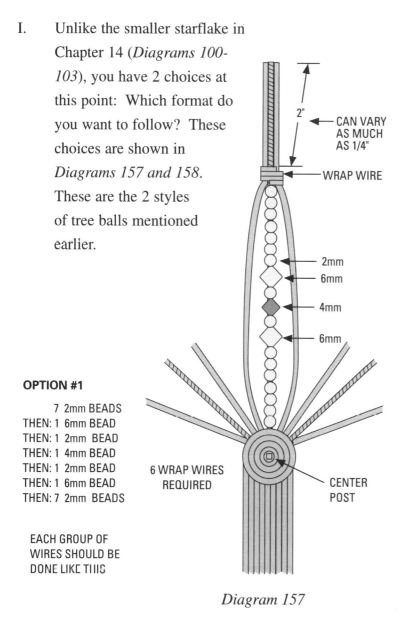

2"
← CAN VARY AS MUCH AS 1/4"

← WRAP WIRE

2mm
6mm

4mm

6mm

OPTION #1

7 2mm BEADS
THEN: 1 6mm BEAD
THEN: 1 2mm BEAD
THEN: 1 4mm BEAD
THEN: 1 2mm BEAD
THEN: 1 6mm BEAD
THEN: 7 2mm BEADS

6 WRAP WIRES REQUIRED

CENTER POST

EACH GROUP OF WIRES SHOULD BE DONE LIKE THIS

Diagram 157

OPTION #2
12 WRAP WIRES REQUIRED

2"

NOTE:
ALL WRAP WIRE **ENDS** ARE THE SAME SIDE AS THE WRAP WIRE CENTER POST

3/4"

CENTER POST

Diagram 158

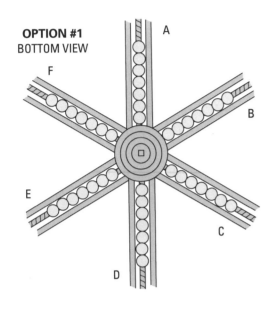

OPTION #1
BOTTOM VIEW

Diagram 159

J.   All **6** arms of this giant starflake must be "beaded up" and wrapped before the next step begins.

K.   The arms must also be spaced evenly around the bottom (base of the center post) wrap wire cover after Step J is completed. *See Diagram 159.*

L.   When all 6 "arms" of the starflake are beaded and tied, the real fun begins! A reminder too: Option #1 can only be used on ROUND tree balls.

M.   From the top wrap wire you should have at least 2" of wire left—DO NOT cut off any. Measure 1" above the wrap wire and bend all three wires back in the opposite direction about 120 degrees. *See Diagram 160.*

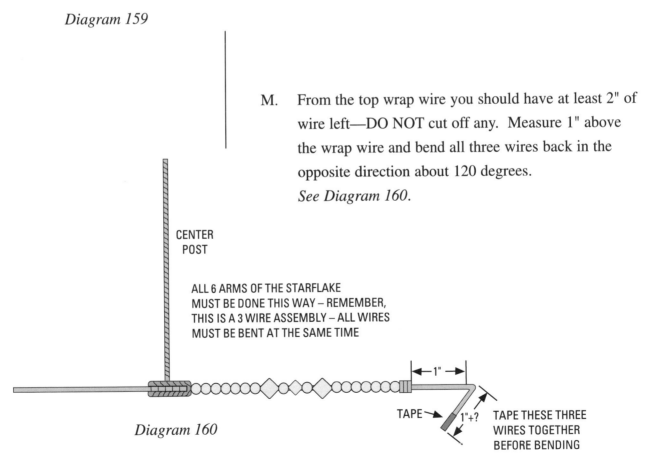

CENTER
POST

ALL 6 ARMS OF THE STARFLAKE
MUST BE DONE THIS WAY – REMEMBER,
THIS IS A 3 WIRE ASSEMBLY – ALL WIRES
MUST BE BENT AT THE SAME TIME

TAPE

TAPE THESE THREE
WIRES TOGETHER
BEFORE BENDING

Diagram 160

N.   **All round** tree balls (whether Option #1 or Option #2) are done this way.

O.   Using the flat nose, grip the beaded arm near the base of the center post (gently) and bend up slightly. Move the pliers up the entire arm at 1/4" intervals and bend up very slightly. The result will be a semicircle beginning at the base of the center post, then arching out and coming back to the center post. *See Diagram 161.* The bending process should follow in this order: *(See Diagram 160)* "A" then "D"/ "F" then "C"/ "B" then "E".

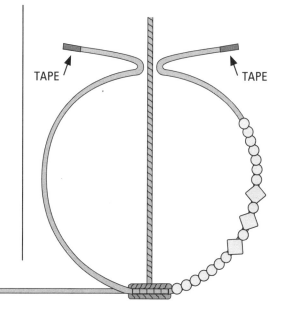

Diagram 161

P.   To make sure that this tree ball is as symmetrical (round) as possible, make sure each arm, after being bent, is level at the top with each of the other arms.

Q.   You may now fill the center post with any bead arrangement you choose. You can match the beads in the arms or contrast them. Do not put more than 1 or 2 beads beyond the point where the 6 arms come together at the center post.

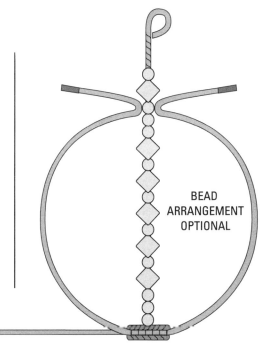

Diagram 162

R.   Put a loop in the top of the center post so the beads will not slip off.

S.   Continue making this loop until it is down to the bead on the center post.

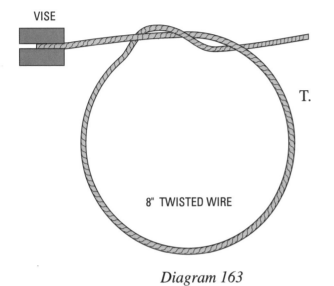

Diagram 163

T. Using the 8" twisted piece, put one end in the vise and make an overhand knot in the wire but DO NOT pull it tight. See *Diagram 163*.

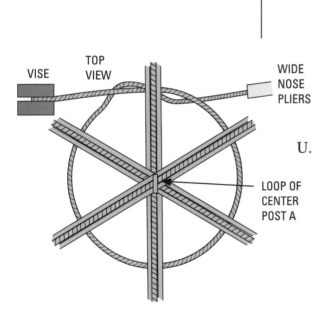

Diagram 164

U. Put the bent over arms in the loop (you can do this by tilting the ball). When all are completely in the loop, pull the twisted wire gently until the loop is closed securely around all 6 groups of wire and the center post. Keep in mind the 6 groups of wires must be directly over the beads they are holding. When the loop is closed tightly, it should stay put for the next procedure. *See Diagrams 164 and 165*. You may wrap it around the previous loop and pull it tight again.

V. The group wires in *Diagram 160*, page 146 must now be bent 180 degrees (from 120 degrees). Continue to bend them so they lie against the beads, and with the wide nose pliers, squeeze them gently so they stay put and are snug. The loop wire (G and H) in *Diagram 166* can now be used to stabilize the tree ball.

W. Bring wire "G" back over group wires "F" and put it back under group wires "F" and then under group wires "E", then back over group wires "E", then under group wires "E", then under group wires "D". Wrap around group wires "D" twice and then cut the end off underneath.

X. Bring wire "H" back over group wires "A" and put it back under group wires "A" and then under group wires "B", then back over group wires "B" and then under group wires "C", then back over group wires "C" twice and cut off underneath. Wires G and H must be as close to the center post as possible. They must be snug and tight. Finished tie down *Diagram 167*. This is the process by which **all** tree balls are secured (teardrop, square or round). The teardrop is, by far, the most difficult, but it can be done. If you can do one of these in under 3 hours, consider yourself an accomplished wirewrapper.

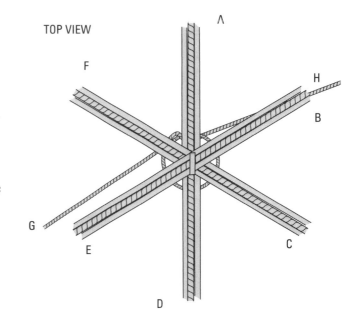

Diagram 166

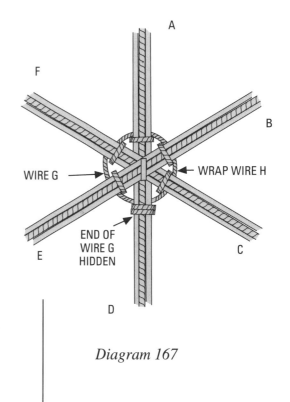

Diagram 167

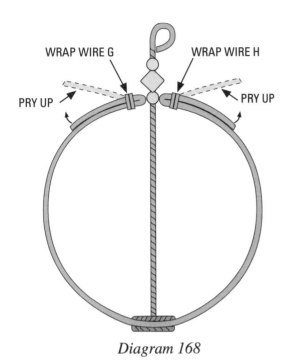

WRAP WIRE G   WRAP WIRE H

PRY UP   PRY UP

Diagram 168

Y. Pry up, with a wide blade pocket knife, all 18 wires of groups A, B, C, D, E, F and spread them. Six of them are already twisted; twist the other 12 with the pin vise. *See Diagram 168* for the pry up.

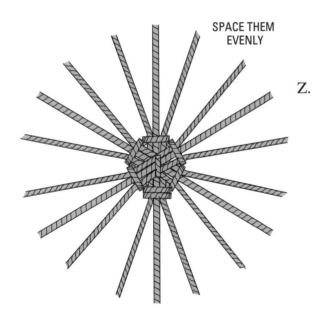

SPACE THEM
EVENLY

Diagram 169

Z. Each group wire can now be swirled into a flat disk and placed specifically. There is a center wire, a left wire, and a right wire to each set of group wires. After they are made into flat disks, they are placed directly over the wires of their original group—left , center, and right. The wires should be long enough so the 3 swirls over each of the group wires should cover up the tie down wire (G and H).

AA. The final step is putting on the hanging hook. Put a jump ring on the loop of the center post, then attach a hook to the jump ring. *See Diagram 170.*

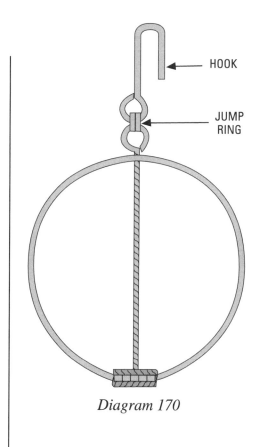

HOOK

JUMP RING

Diagram 170

SUMMARY:

For a look at the finished product, take note of the color pictures in this book. There are other variations not shown here. The directions for the teardrop, square, and round tree balls are all the same. The only difference is in the shape. There is a pear-shaped one done with only 6 wires. The wires are filled with alternating 3mm copper and cobalt blue 4mm beads done up in silver wire.

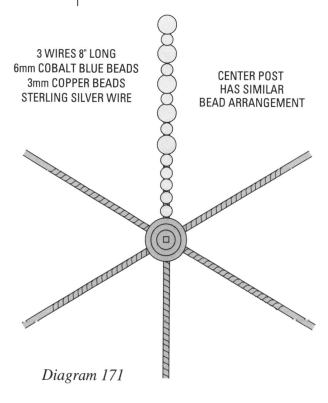

3 WIRES 8" LONG
6mm COBALT BLUE BEADS
3mm COPPER BEADS
STERLING SILVER WIRE

CENTER POST
HAS SIMILAR
BEAD ARRANGEMENT

Diagram 171

CHAPTER 19 CHRISTMAS TREE BALLS

For earrings, there is also one made with three 3" wires (gold-filled), then each wire is filled with ten 2mm sterling silver beads and tied together the same as the tree ball—they are about 1" in diameter. There is an infinite variety of design and the one I have had the most comment on is an all wire one with no beads. Rather than each arm having a bead arrangement, each arm has a sterling silver snowflake, and the center post has a large snowflake. The entire tree ball is made of 22 GA **twisted** gold-filled wire. Each wrap wire has its own wrap wire cover (there are 20 wrap wire covers!) *See Diagram 172.*

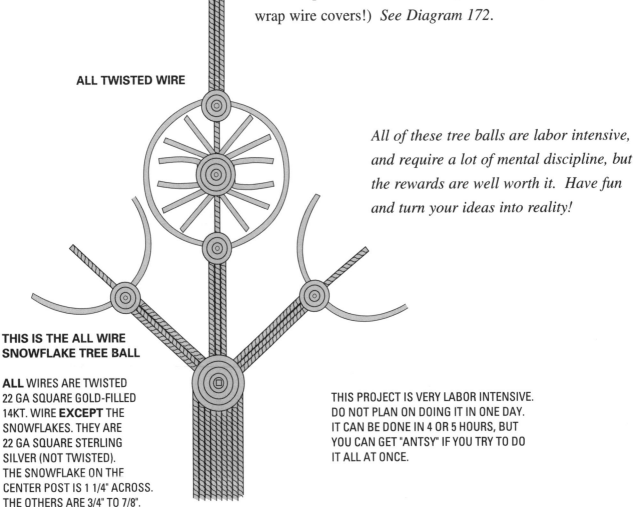

ALL TWISTED WIRE

All of these tree balls are labor intensive, and require a lot of mental discipline, but the rewards are well worth it. Have fun and turn your ideas into reality!

**THIS IS THE ALL WIRE
SNOWFLAKE TREE BALL**

ALL WIRES ARE TWISTED
22 GA SQUARE GOLD-FILLED
14KT. WIRE **EXCEPT** THE
SNOWFLAKES. THEY ARE
22 GA SQUARE STERLING
SILVER (NOT TWISTED).
THE SNOWFLAKE ON THE
CENTER POST IS 1 1/4" ACROSS.
THE OTHERS ARE 3/4" TO 7/8".

THIS PROJECT IS VERY LABOR INTENSIVE.
DO NOT PLAN ON DOING IT IN ONE DAY.
IT CAN BE DONE IN 4 OR 5 HOURS, BUT
YOU CAN GET "ANTSY" IF YOU TRY TO DO
IT ALL AT ONCE.

Diagram 172

If you want to put a small angel in a tree ball, it is very easy to do. Before you make the wrap wire and cover, just add two 2" wires before you put on this wrap wire. *See Diagrams 173 and 174.*

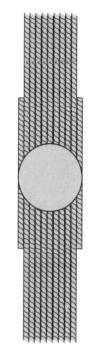

THESE TWO SHORT WIRES ON EITHER SIDE CAN BE USED TO ATTACH AN ANGEL INSIDE OF THE TREE BALL

Diagram 173

With such a variety of bead arrangements available for the tree balls and starflakes, this book has only scratched the surface of what can be done. Even though the step-by-step diagrams shown in this book are extremely important, they are of little value unless you are willing to spend many hours practicing the fine art of wirewrapping.

Try to discipline yourself to be PATIENT and you will be an exceptional wirewrapper! AND DON'T EVER STOP PRACTICING!

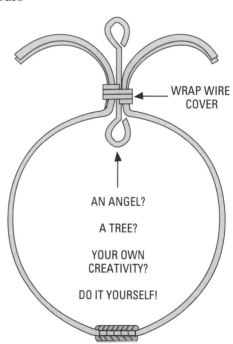

WRAP WIRE COVER

AN ANGEL?

A TREE?

YOUR OWN CREATIVITY?

DO IT YOURSELF!

Diagram 174

EPILOGUE

This book has introduced a new tool (the twister pliers) and a new variety of wire (magnet wire–square and round). As you have gone through the projects in this book, it has become quite apparent to you that a new level of wirewrapping is just beginning to emerge.

There are as many new horizons to be explored as there are people who have the imagination and the patience to explore them. Don't ever underestimate your innerself by saying "I can't!" Challenge yourself and say with a positive approach, "I'll try!!!" Soon, trying becomes automatic and failure is no longer an option—beautiful things begin to happen.

"Play" with the wire as often as you can. Soon the wire will become your friend and quickly great things will fall into place. It's almost like a marriage between the wire and your own personality, with your imagination as the best man. This marriage can be blissfully perpetuated by taking a vow of PRACTICE, PERSEVERANCE, and PATIENCE! With this in mind, you cannot help but succeed!

FAREWELL FOR NOW,

AND PERHAPS IN A COUPLE OF YEARS

I'LL MEET YOU AGAIN IN VOLUME IV!

I went down to the shore today . . .

I went down to the shore today.
That's what I thought to do.
I sat right near the water,
And shed a tear for you.

I know you loved the ocean.
I remember walking there,
With you beside my shoulder,
We didn't have a care.

It seems like that was yesterday.
I really never knew,
That I'd cherish one small moment,
And all the others, too.

To let you go would be so hard,
So I dismissed the thought.
And I had to watch you struggle,
So I know how hard you fought.

When it was time for you to leave,
I didn't have such trouble.
You were like a different person.
But now the pain is double.

I try to think of memories
That wouldn't make me sore.
But I was wrong, they make no sense,
To know there won't be more.

How come you've left I do not know.
But I don't ask why.
All I know is that I love you,
And that you had to die.

For my whole life I always knew,
That you were always there.
And now you're gone. See how it's hard?
It doesn't seem so fair.

When I need strength, I look to God,
And try to say that I'm
Still loving you from way down here,
But He's got perfect time.

I know you're watching down on me,
So I want you to hear,
That your family's all O.K. on Earth.
We know you're always near.

I know you always love me.
You know I love you too.
I went down to the shore today,
And shed a tear for you.

Brittany Wiggins
January 1998
(age 13)

156

ED SINCLAIR'S BOOKS AVAILABLE:

Volume I Moods in Wire
ISBN: 0-9640483-0-2

Volume II Moods in Brass and Glass
ISBN: 0-9640483-1-0

Volume III Holiday Moods in Wire
ISBN: 0-9640483-2-9

Video instructional tapes are also available.

To order authentic "Moods in Wire" <u>wire wrap kits</u> *for selected projects designed by E.E. Sinclair, call or write:*
    Rodgers & Nelsen Publishing Co.
    PO Box 7001
    Loveland, CO 80537-0001
    Phone: 1-970-593-9557
    Fax: 1-970-593-9911
    Email: rnpub@aol.com

Special retailer and volume pricing available!

Problems? Need Advice? Write to:
        E. E. Sinclair
        P. O. Box 2011
        Manassas, VA 22110

Please enclose a stamped, self-addressed envelope and your telephone number.

NOTES

NOTES